Namaskar

Selected publications by the author:

POETRY
I Was That Woman (Hippopotamus Press, Frome, 1989; & Writers Workshop, Calcutta, 1997. *Cette Femme Là...*, published by L'Harmattan, Paris, 2000)
The Sun Rises in the North with J Lyons, C Martin & L Sissay (Smith/ Doorstop Books, 1991)
A Little Bridge with Simon Fletcher & Basir Sultan Kazmi (Pennine Pens, Hebden Bridge, 1997)
Albino Gecko (University of Salzburg, 1998)
Animal Antics (Pennine Pens, 2000)
Jade Horse Torso: Poems and Translations (Sixties Press, Sutton, 2003)

EDITING & TRANSLATION
Barbed Lines ed. with Rashida Islam (BWSG Book Project & Yorkshire Art Circus, 1990)
Won the Raymond Williams Community Publishing Prize 1990
Sweet and Sour ed. with Rehana Choudhury, Karabi Ghose & Rashida Islam (BWSG Book Project, Sheffield, 1993)
Northern Poetry Vol. II ed. with William Scammell (Littlewood Arc, Todmorden, 1991)
Home to Home ed. with Safuran Ara & trans. from Bengali (Sheffield Libraries, 1995)
Album by Uma Prasad Mukherjee, trans. with Tara Chatterjee (Writers Workshop, 1997)
The Snake Prince & Other Folk Tales of Bengal ed. with Rehana Choudhury (BWSG Book Project, 1999)
Songs in Exile by Safuran Ara, trans. from Bengali (Sheffield Libraries, 1999)
The Redbeck Anthology of British South Asian Poetry (Redbeck Press, Bradford, 2000)
Won the Raymond Williams Runner-up Prize 2001
Who Cares: Reminiscences of Yemeni Carers in Sheffield (Sheffield Carers Centre, 2001)
My Birth Was Not in Vain: Selected Poems by Seven Bengali Women ed. with Safuran Ara (Sheffield Libraries, 2001)
Nazrul Islam poster-poems and notes (Survivors' Poetry, London, 2001)
Rainbow World: Poems from Many Cultures ed. with Bashabi Fraser (Hodder, London, 2003)
Generations of Ghazals: Ghazals by Nasir Kazmi & Basir Sultan Kazmi (Redbeck Press, 2003; & in Urdu by Maktaba-e-Khayal, Lahore, 2004)
Daughters of a Riverine Land ed. with Ashoka Sen (BWSG Book Project, 2003)
Sixties Press Anthology of Gregory Fellows' Poetry ed. with Barry Tebb (Sixties Press, 2004)

CRITICISM
The Role of Religion in A Passage to India (Writers Workshop, Calcutta, 1984)

FICTION FOR CHILDREN
The Elephant-Headed God & Other Hindu Tales (Lutterworth, Cambridge, 1989; Rupa, India, 1993; Oxford University Press, USA, 1992 & Madras Editora in Portuguese trans., Brazil, 1999)
Nyamia & the Bag of Gold (Longman, 1994)
The Monkey God & Other Hindu Tales (Rupa, India, 1993)
Sufi Stories from Around the World (Harper Collins India, 1994)

PLAYS FOR CHILDREN
The Message of Thunder & Other Plays (Orient Longman, Chennai, 1999)
Plays for Children 2 with David Greig, Mike Kenny & Peter Rumney (Faber & Faber, London, 2004)

Namaskar
NEW AND SELECTED POEMS
by
DEBJANI CHATTERJEE

RED
BECK
PRESS
2004

Namaskar: New and Selected Poems is published by:
Redbeck Press, 24 Aireville Road, Frizinghall
Bradford, BD9 4HH

Printed at the Arc & Throstle Press,
Nanholme Mill, Todmorden, Lancs.

ISBN 1 904338 06 2
First published 2004

**Redbeck Press acknowledges financial assistance
from the Arts Council of England, Yorkshire.**

My pranams to the memory of my Baba
(Sanat Kumar Chatterjee, 1921 – 1994),
my Timarpur Dadu
(Sailendra Nath Chatterjee, 1888 – 1968)
and Bhaloma
(Niharbala Devi, 1904 – 1967),
and my Mussoorie Dadu
(Priyo Nath Mukherjee, 1904 – 1965)
and Dida
(Bashanti Devi, 1915 – 1949).

Acknowledgments

The selected poems are from Debjani Chatterjee's: *I Was That Woman* (Hippopotamus Press, 1989); *Albino Gecko* (University of Salzburg, 1998); and *Jade Horse Torso* (Sixties Press, 2003); and her collections in: *Flame* (Crocus Books, 1991); *The Sun Rises in the North* (Smith/Doorstop Books, 1991); and *A Little Bridge* (Pennine Pens, 1997).

'The Elephant' won the Lancaster Lit-fest Open Poetry Competition, 1988; 'The Parrot Fortune-Teller' and 'To the English Language' were winning entries in the Peterloo Poets Open Poetry Competition 1989; 'Paolozzi's Magic Kingdom' was commissioned by Sheffield's Graves Art Gallery in 1988 and shortlisted for the First Artrage Annual Literature Awards 1989; 'Visiting E M Forster' won Second Prize in the Southport Writers Circle Open Poetry Competition 1992; 'Words Between Us' was Highly Commended in the Bournemouth International Festival Poetry Competition 1992, 'Invitation to the Party' won 'Special Mention' in the Ripley Poetry Competition 1992; 'Koinobori' was commended in the English Explorer Magazine National Poetry Competition 1992; and 'Snips and Snails' was commissioned by the Blue Nose Poets for Freud's birth anniversary, May 1996. 'Jade Horse Torso' and 'Lucrezia's Mirror' are a response to the 'Precious' Exhibition' at Sheffield's Millennium Galleries where Debjani Chatterjee was writer-in-residence in 2001.

Some of the 'new' poems were previously published in: *Fire, Dream Catcher, Daughters of a Riverine Land* (BWSG Book Project, 2003), *Animal Antics* (Pennine Pens, 2000), *Edinburgh: An Intimate City* (The City of Edinburgh Council, 2000), *Drafting and Assessing Poetry: A Guide for Teachers* (Paul Chapman Publishing, 2003), *Muse: Poems Exploring Inspiration* (Poetry Monthly Press, 2002), *Dinos, Dodos and Other Dead Things* (Macmillan, 2003), *Mice on Ice* (Macmillan, 2004) and *Saffron Tea* (Heaventree Press, 2004). 'Interludes' was commissioned for the *Poems for the Waiting Room* project by David Hart and Rogan Wolf in 2000; 'More Than I Wear' was commissioned by Calderdale Museums & Arts Dept. in 2003; and 'Home' was commissioned by the Barbican Centre in 2003. 'Home' and 'Not Goldilocks' are a response to Sebastião Salgado's 'Exodus' exhibition at the Barbican Centre.

Contents

From *I Was That Woman* (1989)

From *Flame* (1991)

From *The Sun Rises in the North* (1991)

From *A Little Bridge* (1997)

From *Albino Gecko* (1998)

From *Jade Horse Torso* (2003)

Namaskar: New Poems

From *I Was That Woman* (1989)

I Was That Woman

At the very beginning of creation
I was dormant, potential, Pandora's box,
a package deal for Adam,
a surprise birthday present
with a time-bomb ticking inside.
He opened me with wonder,
he tasted me with delight.
I was that woman, ashamed and resentful,
wise yet weak, bold but blushing,
with lowered eyes I walked away from Eden
without a backward glance, smouldering.
The first rebel, I was the mother of Cain,
and was punished with pain and servitude.
I was that woman, pure and radiant,
abducted by a demon across the sea;
banished but dutiful, I bore twin kings,
till exhausted at last I cried for the earth.
I was that woman outraged by a hundred,
my modesty a never-ending sari,
while righteous husbands watched in silence,
the handling of their property, the strangling of their pride.

I was the woman of mystery and magic
who sang on the waves and waved my wand
to provide adventures for heroic men on an obstacle course.
I was that beautiful horror with snake-hair,
to be slain with a shudder by the brave.
My crime is that I felt for a fellow victim:
woman-like, I wept for fallen Lucifer.
I was that woman, poor and lowly,
who hid behind a tree and offered
my single garment to the mendicant sage.
I was that woman who tearfully pleaded
and pestered the Compassionate One
to relent and admit me and my kind.
I was that woman who bowed and listened

to Mahavir's message of hope: release
is mine in a next life – as a man!
I was that woman who destroyed my breast
to fight with men on their own ground.
I was that woman of ill repute
who washed those feet with repentant tears,
grateful that he would not lift a stone;
but accepting my untouchable lot.
I was that woman trapped in a brothel,
who cared not for heaven or hell,
but loved Allah in spite of his masculinity.
I was that woman who roused a nation
and was burnt so many times at so many stakes.
I was the woman at whom the Vedas, the Avesta,
the Bible and the Quran were flung;
their God was the bogeyman
who kindly sent male prophets
to keep me humble in my place.

I was that woman, silly and rouged,
of endless chatter, and timeless in dressing,
whose mind is full-blown and scattered with the wind,
whose moods – mysterious like the tides –
fluctuate with the changing moon.
I was that woman whose nude body inspired
while the sculptor appreciated and chiselled.
I was the woman with soul desecrated
who typed away from ten to five with two tea breaks.
I was that woman at the helm of six hundred million,
who longed to be accepted as simply human,
a real person like others, and not a myth.
I was the woman, neurotic, torn, disowning my sex.
I was the voluptuous, decorative drudge.
I was the creature with will power raped.
I was that woman…

Notes
The woman 'abducted by a demon' was Sita, heroine of *The Ramayana*,
daughter of the Earth and mother of the twins Lav and Kush.
The 'woman outraged by a hundred' was Draupadi, heroine of *The
Mahabharata*. Her 'never-ending sari' refers to a miracle when Krishna
rescued her modesty.
The woman who 'pestered the Compassionate One' was the Buddha's aunt
who begged him to allow women to become nuns.
Mahavir ('the Great Hero'), also called Vardhamana, is regarded as the greatest
teacher of Jainism. Jainism was founded in the 6th Century B.C. in revolt
against the ritualism of Hinduism at that time. Jains are so respectful of all life
(*ahimsa*) that they will not kill even the smallest insect.

Holding On

I do not know if he was a sage,
nor if he was a philosopher.
I only know that he sat cross-legged,
silent on the sand by the river.

'Tell me the meaning of life,' I begged.
He smiled and answered me not a word.
'I'll not leave empty-handed,' I said.
He smiled and I wondered if he heard.

Exasperated, I made to go
when he smiled and gathered up some sand.
As he turned and looked into my eyes,
he let it trickle from his hand.

Uncertainly I pulled out my purse.
(Had he somehow answered after all?)
Hesitant, I gave a rupee note.
He smiled and slowly let it fall.

The Parrot Fortune-Teller

On the streets of Delhi, in my childhood,
I came across parrot fortune-tellers.
Their miserable keepers did not count:
in drab poverty served, but hardly owned
the treasures toiling in their dingy midst.
You gave a meagre coin, though such knowledge
cannot be bought – so some eke a living.

With coaxing words the prophet would strut out
of its cage, bobbing green head and flicking
disdainful tail, pecking at alphabets
which spelt out the customer's destiny.
Something impersonal in its eye, this
captive creature's beak and claws contained clues
to catapult you. While you contemplate

marriage, children, jobs, examinations,
robberies and suicide, how dare it
dream of raw chillies and chick peas? It needs
to fly, you need to fly from silly games.
But that's why you go to the parrot
fortune-teller, isn't it? It revolves
and slowly waddles back through the trap-door.

Recollecting Youth

O jasmine garland,
wilted in white hair, you scent
my memories green.

The Question

Being Indian, I live abroad
in England, Germany, Disneyland,
wherever my rainbow spirit beckons.
I have inherited the earth.
In the world's metropolises
I mount my escalating destiny.
The loneliness of city jungles
shelters the reluctant immigrant
amid skyscraper towers of silence.
I roam the mugger-stalked streets
of Porno-Babel, an easy victim,
unwelcome on the gold and tinsel pavements,
but free to go my way.
The indifferent air of rooftop
car parks and rush hour subways
strengthens me and gives me space
to grow and remove my mask.

But on annual pilgrimage
my jet-hopping brings me back
to old and sentimental melodies.
India is a warm invitation
to rest myself – on a bed of nails.
The question is: 'Do I embrace the thorns
for the elusive scent of the mystic rose?'
I skirt my way through throbbing bazaars,
a feast for flies and charlatans,
butted by bulls and pot-bellied *banias*,
oozing sores and gleaming bangles
fashioned of ephemeral dreams,
saffron, vermilion, cow-dung, sacred mud …
'Am I in this, or is this part of me?
Does the lotus unfold within me
and am I its muddy bed?'

In defining my Indian-ness
I can only unravel the essential me.
Here every slimy ditch aspires to be the Ganges,
the smelly pickpockets have the impish smile
of the immortal butter thief.
India prostrates me with its heady atmosphere.
My eyes close in sandalwood and billowing sari *pallavs*.
The sun beats down like no other sun.
How can one resist the rhythm of the rain,
the chatter of parrots, the calling temple bells,
and the cinnamon cloud of evening dust?
They spread like *maya* over my vision.
So I must escape this gentle mocking love,
if only to be able to ponder my question…

Notes
bania: a merchant.
'The immortal butter thief' refers to Gopala – Krishna as a child.
pallav: the end of the sari which hangs down over the shoulder.
maya: maya is variously interpreted as illusion, ignorance and delusion. It is also
the creative and transforming power of God, especially in God's feminine aspect.

Nazrul

As loved ones died around you,
your mind and body parted.
Your poetry, strong on every lip,
bore no connection to the practice
of the world at large around you.
In the midst of brothers and sisters
you found yourself bereft, bereaved.
By what right do your people claim you?

Your cyclone voice swept the nation,
a typhoon tore through prison bars:
you were Muslim, you were Hindu,
a prophet of the Motherland
that breathed so fiercely in your dreams.

Your brave cry stifled, alas,
when madness shrouded the land.
The giant screamed, the Himalayas shook,
blood thundered in rivers and in your ears.
Partition hung like a vulture-cloud:
dismembered ones wailed as they were born.
Your mind and body parted,
as loved ones died around you.

Note
Nazrul Islam, 'the Rebel Poet of Bengal', ranks with Tagore as one of modern
India's greatest poets. His songs and poems inspired the movement for freedom
from British rule. He married a Hindu and passionately believed in Hindu-
Muslim solidarity in a united Bengal. He was heartbroken at witnessing the
communal tension and violence when Bengalis killed one another. Before India's
'Partition' in 1947, he had already suffered a major breakdown and remained
speechless and unproductive for the rest of his life. When East Pakistan became
independent Bangladesh, Nazrul was honoured as its national poet.

The Elephant

Elephants were not her cup of tea –
they were mammoth and boring,
immobile, they turned no somersaults.
Gaiety and the antics of monkeys
and insulting parakeets,
blinking and chattering,
offered her the warmth of fur and vivid feathers.
Elephants were distant, tusked and ominous.
Powerful and towering over children,
their long memories and wisdom
placed them in a different zoo – for adults.
'But this is an Indian elephant,'
her father said. 'It is homesick
and will cheer up to see an Indian girl
in this wet, cold, foreign land.'
So she tore away from the noisy cages
and allowed herself to be slowly led
to greet her majestic compatriot.
She avoided those massive tree trunk legs
and looked straight up at the eyes.
A storehouse of sorrow was locked in its brain.
Tentative, she reached out and patted
the incredible trunk stretched out to her.

On the Centenary of Edward Lear's Death

June 6th, 1988 – and Poet's Corner
in Westminster Abbey, London, created room
for a nonsense king, the celebrated author
of Yonghy-Bonghy-Bo. Roll on the tourist boom!
The mighty literati shuffled in slightly.
Thrilled to have company, Lewis carolled a whoop,
unfamiliar laughter in that hallowed sanctum:
in the cobbled aisle the pobble had won a coup.
Even Prince Charles had sent a letter to support
the poet-cartoonist who was drawing master
to his famous we-are-not-amused ancestor,
sponsoring his gaining entry to Westminster
a century after his death. Even the Dean
declared himself 'extremely pleased' for limericks
to run riot in his cathedral. When questioned
if the Creator ever engaged in frolics,
he said that they were a part of human nature.
Lear's memorial stone erected resembled
another beside it to poets sacrificed
in the First World War. As the world assembled,
a Lear expert and biographer pronounced:
'Straightforward cheer'. How pleasant to know Mr Lear!
'The British, as a nation,' she philosophised,
'do not take their humour seriously, I fear.'

Animal Regalia

"For the launch of our modest exhibition,
we need an expert on animal regalia,"
announced the enthusing gallery person.
"Just a small audience, only local media –
you volunteered to make a contribution –
even ten minutes on animal regalia
from you will sound authentic, gain attention,
and spiced snacks can be ordered from the Light of Asia,"
purred the telephone voice in expectation.
I longed to plead a sudden total amnesia.
Well, I work in community relation,
so you think me a walking encyclopaedia
on saris, *surma*, steel bands, circumcision,
calypso, kosher, carnival bacchanalia,
reggae, ragas, Rastas, race, revolution,
multi-culturalese, sickle cell anaemia,
equal opportunities, deportation,
halal meat, Hinduism, hunger, third world hernia,
visas, arranged marriages, immigration,
ethnic monitoring and paraphernalia.
I should be used now to this phenomenon,
but confessed surprise at animal regalia
and duly pleaded lack of all connection.
"But elephants, horses, camels come from India,
just like you!" came the logical assumption.
Well, so they do. I begin to get the idea!

Note
surma: kohl

A Pea-Sized Impediment

Princess, I read that you were pleased
to put up with their stupid tests.
The Queen did try to put you off
from marrying that prize prince.
His own mother! That should have warned you.
But you had to have him.
So she thought up impossible
feats for you to perform
and you rose to the challenge,
like some royal seal performing a trick.
Under mountains of mattresses
was a pea-sized impediment
to test the delicate nature
of your regal imperfection.
Predictably you tossed and groaned
and did not sleep a wink,
thereby proving yourself a princess.
Is this really all it takes?
You won the prize, alright: your prince.
But it wasn't till you retired
to the test of the bridal bed,
that you discovered that you were two –
two pea-sized impediments in a pod.

Reflection

Grandparents sit with children,
still, for once, on their knees,
all smiling, all smart,
in the sunshine garden.
Captured for posterity
is all that family togetherness,
the sense that we go on forever.
My shy cousin leaning her plaited head
on the grand wicker armchair,
is married now to a business tycoon.
The spoilt little one looks up
from kohl-fringed eyes
and shows off his fire engine, painted red
and unique in the neighbourhood
for its strident sound.
My sensible brother stands at the edge
but still manages to give the impression
that he is herding us children in.
My sister's expression of concentration
is the same one I often see
on my nephew doing homework –
there's a faint look of anxious-to-get-away
and I remember all the adventures
of that garden just beyond the picture frame:
the 'crocodile and bank' game we played,
especially hilarious in monsoon weather;
the temple worship for which we gathered
flowers, leaves and stones,
taking it in turn to be head priest,
and how carefully we observed the rule
about removing our sandals and canvas shoes;
we played at patriots too and drove out the British
again and again…
My grandfather is sitting ramrod straight,
the head of the house, a self-made man

with a title from the Raj for services
rendered a war-time Ministry of Defence.
His patrician nose on a stern brown face
belies the warm and gentle eyes.

My grandmother sports the largest red dot
on her forehead and her round face
beams her pleasure, her gusto in life.
A red-bordered white sari drapes her head,
a handsome woman, full of strength.
I am standing self-conscious
and holding up the lacy new frock
so that the knickers peep at the camera.
Somewhere in the middle of the picture
I am posing and doing my duty.

Flamingos

Flamingo flying –
Coral splashed on watery
Mountains and slate skies.

Flamingos flooding
A lake with koi carp swimming
Amidst bright water.

Flamingos flying –
Corals splashed with careless hand
Over burnished skies.

Transfiguration

Waiting, I count the seasons, the dewdrops on grass;
waiting through heavy centuries, the aeons pass.
Heroes are born to live and die, reincarnate,
while I remain the same, a thing of stone. I wait,
anaesthetised in my fossilised extinction.
Fellow beast, in your raging mask of revulsion,
you rant and kick at me for lying in your sight,
howl your frustration as your Beauty takes fright,
denying you love in her inability
to penetrate your animal nobility.
Werewolf, baying the moon, you don't suffer alone.
At your feet cant you sniff the blood inside my stone?
This is a jungle of the accursed. Look around.
Am I inanimate, a nothing on the ground?
You little know the cracks in the centre where veins
of frozen tears swell like suspended winter rains.
I count the footfalls – Frog, hopping on my shame,
are you too silenced, playing an enchanter's game?
Speckled belly that slithers, squeezing me slantwise,
are you owned by some freckled Snake-Prince in disguise?
I listen for the difference – how will I know
His blessed step when the moment comes? Whose shadow,
like a mantle of compassion, will liberate?
I anticipate his coming, I celebrate.
In what distant land is born the incarnation
who will some day effect my transfiguration?
When will it be known that I have learnt my lesson
and am fit again to take my place in Heaven?
Do the beautiful ones recall me in their sport?
It seems a dream that I once danced in Indra's court.
That celestial nymph is no longer in history,
the earth's alchemy has wrought its own mystery
and made of me an ageless rock. I cannot act,
I do not move, I only am. But it is fact:
I am not stone, I am evolving. Oh I swear

I am not the same. Even in this granite snare,
my pinioned wings are slowly gathering force
in readiness to shatter this shell of remorse.
I wait for one who will raise me from the abyss;
I am changed. It is time to keep his promise.

Notes
'Snake-Prince': a popular character in Indian fairy tales.
Indra: Indra is Svargapati, 'the Lord of Heaven'.

To the English Language

Indifferent language of an alien shore,
the journey was troubled but I am here:
register me among your step-children.

That special love that flows easy with my birthright
is for Bengali, my mother – a well rounded tongue,
sweet and juicy with monsoon warmth,
rich and spicy with ancestral outpourings.

What has proficiency to do with it?
I know I dream it endlessly.

English, your whiplash of thoughts
has scarred me, pebbles rattle in my mouth
while innuendoes turn my tongue.

For generations you called to me,
siren of the seven western seas,
though now you may deny this and tell me
to go back where I came from.
Your images were the barbed lines
that drew me, torn, to this island keep.

Your words raise spectral songs to haunt me.
I have subverted your vocabulary
and mined rebellious corridors of sound.
I have tilled the frozen soil of your grammar
– I will reap the romance of your promises.

I know you now
with the persistence that a stranger musters.
I know the madness hidden in your rules and relics,
I see the glory where you would disown it.
I know my own desperate yearning,
but I do not come to your rhythms empty-handed
– the treasures of other traditions are mine,
so many koh-i-noors, to be claimed.

It is now my turn to call you at my homecoming.
I have learnt to love you
– the hard way.

Note
Koh-i-noor: a famous Indian diamond that is now a British crown jewel.

Lowest Common Denominator

Lord, you told us: 'Go forth and multiply.'
Did you think you could manipulate us?
      But we are contrary creatures:
      We've been dividing ever since.
You reckoned without us calculators.

By the Wayside

It should not be broken against the skull;
it should bring a smile to your face, not tears.

Buy one for its verdant beauty, its firm smooth skin,
curve your hands around the voluptuous oval,
breathe in its tangy vibrant scent of woodland grove,
lift it in your palm, feel the luscious weight:
bigger is better, heavier more heavenly.
Shake it about and the swirling pool will whisper
promises, once released.

Then bargain with the vendor who already knows
that you must have it. Wait by the wayside for him
to strike at its crown in slicing petal patterns
and to decapitate it with a single blow
of his blade, and so present you, with a flourish,
liquid delectation.

It is the milk of natural kindness.
Drink in the tropics, waving seas, palm trees,
and stillness sliding down your sun-drenched throat
till the last caressing drop is possessed.

Then watch the knife descend in cleaving strokes
dissecting inner walls and so reveal
the white flesh – inviting, ripe for biting.

Dig deeply and scrape it from the shell, and savour
the succulent serendipity, the flavour
of earthy fantasy. Its flesh is sensuous:
a chewy cool delight.

A feast for sight and palate: meal complete,
a coconut is nature's milk and meat.

Alamgir

Soothsayers warned your grandsire, Jahangir.
Uneasy, he sought to placate you –
too late – with the terrible gift of Alamgir,
the sharp sword that you wielded
with ruthless piety and divided
Hindu from Musulman, Shia from Sunni.
But Alamgir was also your title and your tongue
whose single utterance spelt annihilation
to fortune-tellers and all their blasphemy.

No one could have foreseen
that the pale, intense and sickly prince,
forgotten in the middle of so much royalty,
out of place like a pariah surrounded by pomp
and despising the wasteful chatter of
sycophants and courtesans,
storing away the secrets of court intrigues,
closeted with Quran and theologians
who inspired a wild hankering for a dervish life
stifled by a soldier's rough discipline
and crowned by a martyr's lust for duty,
would make the sacrifices that you made
to spread the word of Allah,
extend the domain of Islam,
restore the dynasty to its rightful mission
by bearing the illustrious burden
that made you, in your thirty-ninth year,
the sixth Shahinshah of Hindustan.

Seated on the peacock throne, you wielded stern justice
to enemies who would not, or could not, see your way,
criminals, heathens and madmen in their revelry,
brothers and sons corrupted by glitter and debauchery,
artists and saints who thought to imitate the Creator,
all who put other things before the *Sunna*,

till you dared not ask yourself how many of the *ulema*
were true slaves of Allah, besides yourself.
Like Timur and Genghis, your distant ancestors,
you made of yourself a scourge of Heaven.
Your guard never slipped, but did you confess
in some coded diary or a private prayer,
that you too were a man who had failed?
Was there never a moment of doubt
to shake your understanding of the Truth?

When you left the durbar and its majesty,
Alamgir, tyrant, champion of the faith,
you became an old austere calligrapher,
retired to your monastic cell and plying
your leisure, earning your living, painstakingly
transcribing the divine word in Arabic,
page after memorised page;
your gnarled hands, for variety, skilfully adorning
prayer caps with wholesome immaculate stitches.
You shunned the coffers of the treasury
but they paid for waging wars to promote the peace of Islam.
Yes, enigmatic emperor, the example you set
commanded respect and hate and fear,
but love still eludes you.
Your subjects, like your children, simmered in rebellion.
With dance and music in suspense,
a broken and catatonic nation awaited the long slow death
of the Shahinshah of Hindustan.

Notes
Alamgir: a title of Aurangzeb (1658-1707), the sixth Mughal emperor, Shahjahan's
son and the last of the Great Mughals. Alamgir was also the name of a sword
presented to Aurangzeb by his grandfather, Jahangir.
Shia: the sect of Islam that accepts Ali as the first Caliph.
Sunni: 'those who follow the *sunna* or tradition'. Sunnis are the orthodox, or
main body of Islam.
ulema: Muslim theologians.

31

I Remembered Cinderella

'The Chinese are strange,
they have these fetishes about women:
that's why they bound their feet, forced them to take
tiny mincing steps,'
I was told and I
swallowed this half-lie.
But I remembered Cinderella then.
I considered the tiny mincing steps
she must have taken, dancing with the prince.
(Didn't the little mermaid also feel
she stepped on daggers, dancing with the prince?)
I thought of the test with the glass slippers
which would not fit the large assertive feet
of the wicked and ugly step-sisters.
None in the land was beautiful enough
to own such small feet:
clearly none in the land was the right stuff
to wed the king-to-be.
But, I say, no woman deserved the fate
of prancing with that dunce in the first place!
(What large feet you have, wicked step-sisters!
All the better to kick you with, my dears!)
No, my brothers and my sisters, that land
of powerful myth that has swept many
shores is not China.
I realised then
that it is men
who have fetishes
about women.

Yama

Yama, when my hour comes,
I know you will be there:
solemn, dark and steadfast,
your buffalo pawing
the ground. You are waiting.
I will gladly follow.
I am certain of you,
at least, in this restless
world of humanity.
The sheet you'll wrap around
me is your cloak of peace.
You have gone through this mill
before me,
led so many brothers
and sisters after you,
so you will guide me too.
Yama, when my hour comes,
I know you'll not fail me.
But tell me,
Yama, when your time came,
who came to steer you to
the land that is now yours?
I will gladly follow
you, Guru, on that one
condition.

Note
Yama was the first human to die and thus became the King of the Underworld and God of Death. He is also called Dharmaraj or King of Justice. In Hindu iconography, Yama rides a black buffalo and carries a noose.

Mother Image

Holding her sari, I followed quietly,
I stood in a kitchen corner and watched
her activity – always busy and bustling –
the lynch-pin of our home and lives.
Whenever she sat down with knitting
or a plate of rice or lentils to carefully clean,
I settled on the carpet, nestling by her.
Mother was lavender scent and softness.
Now she's a grandmother,
I watch her: how small she is,
an ageless beauty I can't define.
Did I cause those tired lines
of pain and laughter criss-crossed?
I see myself and our little ones in her
as I watch her with the eyes of love.

Hong Kong Arrival

I grabbed the railing with nervous hands,
propelled into the harbour
looming with its sampan forest,
its spit-flecked blue billowed with bobbing
brown and multi-hued moths and butterflies,
its salted air tangy with fresh melodies.
Tall aspiring buildings hugged the hillside,
shadowing the sea, while painted pagodas
floated ruby, gold and jade.
Overhead the seagulls circled
the traffic plying between Victoria and Kowloon
and all the seas and continents of the world.

Poem in the Post

A glance at the bought postcard
and glib phrases reappear:
'having a wonderful time...
sun 'n sand... wish you were here...
          love....'
No, I will not send to you
postcards for acquaintances
to be treated to envied
suntanned holiday instances.
          Love,
I shall send you a vision
of our future together,
I shall post you a poem:
crystallised perfume of rare
          love.

Ganapati

Parvati, because you loved us, you bade us love the world a little.
Radiant goddess of the mountains, you married the outcast god
                              who haunted cemeteries.
We saw that we should embrace the children of two races:
they are the strong links of connection and bear your blessing,
they are rainbows spanning gulfs of silence, swamps of
                              intolerance.
You wanted to stretch our notions of humanity.
Mother, you lifted your baby son to raise our eyes.
He might have been a monster, were he not a god.
Certainly he was a dimpled rollicking infant
balancing an elephant head with a giant, sweet tusk.
All the world loves a baby – we grew to adore
his enormous belly and appetite, his great animal head,

the wide ears flapping to our songs of praise,
the mobile trunk accepting our wholesome offerings,
the bead-red eyes beaming creature compassion.
We accepted that the brain within the massive skull
was more than animal, human or divine – all wisdom.
He personified a bond that we knew was powerful.
You announced that this, your son, was Ganapati,
the people's Lord, and to be shared with the animals;
you told us that he was the remover of all obstacles.
He was a hero we could live with: we told of his adventures,
laughed at his foibles, we worshipped him.
Your son grew up. Would he marry a goddess like you?
He smiled his solemn elephant smile.
Would he marry an earthly maid, or some animal perhaps?
Ganapati, because he loved us, he bade us love the world a little.
Radiant god, he married the bashful banana tree with its veil
                                    of fertile leaves.
You celebrated this union and gave your blessing.
All the world loves a bride – we joined in and draped
our friend's elegant wife in a red bordered sari, we blew
                                    conch shells.
We stretched our notions of humanity.

Note
Ganapati: Ganapati means 'Lord of the Ganas', the ganas being demi-gods who
attend on Ganapati's father Shiva. He is also popularly called Ganesh or Ganesa
('God of the Ganas'), and is the god of wisdom and good fortune. He is also the
god of Literature and, as 'remover of obstacles', he is invoked at the start of new
undertakings. His elephant head has earned him the epithet Gajanan ('Elephant-
face').

From *Flame* (1991)

Khitish

Hurtling into the clutter-room
whose door hung loose on its hinges,
I knocked against him coming out,
barefoot and with *lungi* folded
above the knees. Khitish held me
with his bony grip and brown eyes,
our lanky servant who was king
of the fish ponds and muddy swamps,
the hero who opened the gates
to adventure. I looked at him
expectantly, for he always
gave me keys that unlock treasures
to scatter in my clutter-room.
From out his pocket a carved top
of sal wood with a string spiralled
tight around it, transferred itself
to my greedy hands. 'All it wants
is a lick of paint,' said Khitish,
'then watch it spin, little sister.'
I twirled it straight away, pulling
back the string with all the flourish
of some conjuror whisking off
a table cloth to leave behind
crockery and cutlery set
in immaculate arrangement.
'Brilliant!' I breathed, giving him
my unstinted admiration.

Note
lungi: material worn wrapped about the waist.

Rhinoceros

To view you is to hurtle back
      a millennium or more.
      Can you and I co-exist
in any time, in any place?

      Hide-clad warrior, risen
      from prehistoric legend,
you stand solid on shifting ground;
      your twin horns, like two upthrust
      thorn fingers, are confronting
our noisy civilization.

Plate on plate of slate-rock beauty,
      impenetrable and mute;
      your poker eyes glaze at us
      within the muddy pockets
to which we relegated you.

      Targeted by winking men
      with bullets and cameras,
      your survival now hinges
      on a blink of history.
Those wrinkled eyes look fossil-closed,
      but the mobile mouth appears
stretched in a Mona Lisa grin.

Something Stirred

Let's relish the kitchen table poems:
peeled layers of scored revelation;
their sliced precision of words, hard and soft;
subtle hint of turmeric in the air.
Soap bubbles catch the moment and the sun;
the ordered menu of kaleidoscope;
twist of pepper added, wand-stirred to life –
work of everyday poets, home-makers.

Ipso Facto

It is a fact that
most people despair
below the breadline.

It is a fact that:
'the world is unfair'
won't make a headline.

It is a fact that
we near the deadline.
Does anyone care?

If so; facto?

Making Waves

Newsflash: 'Britain's no longer an island.'
The ears pricked up at the late night telly.
Only connect to this sceptred isle, land
of European solidarity.
Euro-speak is now the *lingua franca*.
The year rushes to link with a new one
of wall-to-wall breaking perestroika
and Channel Tunnel digging to '91.

Linked to Europe, we're linked to Africa,
to Asia. So welcome, Britain, to the world!
A night for counting Welsh sheep cavorting
sleepless over Euro butter-mountains.
Morning: a flooding sea of commuters
pouring from the station. Hadn't they heard?
But each one travelled with stiff upper lip
Bridges drawn up as they wade through the waves.

From *The Sun Rises in the North* (1991)

Paolozzi's Magic Kingdom

You just enter it and suddenly – you're lost.
No, don't expect to spend a pleasant afternoon:
you won't idle away an hour or two munching
a lazy sandwich, yawning a cup of tea,
glazing at the décor propping up in symmetry
the usual pillars of commercial artistry.
Throw away the price tags of Harrods and Sotheby's.
Didn't the publicity warn you this exhibition
was fiendishly combined to split your mind?

Bite on the bullets of memory, tossed,
pelletted unremittingly with a loving obsession,
again and again, plundered and lost.
This bin kingdom is a magic wasteland
presided over by a skeleton jangling
on a key chain, shorn of dignity and sham;
a rubbish dump overrun by flies, cockroaches, snails,
spiders, scorpions, copulating crickets and butterflies,
where tawdry frogs on cracked mirrors croak fairy tales.
This nightmare catalogues
all that is lost and all that is found;
the power of hidden springing surprises,
the toy-maker, child, primeval artist,
the sculptor, scientist, magpie, rag-and-bones man,
the savage who is hunter, arch-sorcerer, death's head,
out of context, out of time, objects
that are subjects of a strange affinity,
skulls, and weapons civilized,
dredged from aboriginal resources –

the fake reality cheek by jowl with the reality of fakes.

Nothing lives or dies in this kingdom,
but is metamorphosed, cannibalised.
The accoutrements of cultures, centuries and fetishes

press down, stratified with mud and humour,
a lick of paint, a flick of glitter,
history pitfalled with follies,
sermons of silly profundities,
white man's burden, black man's inheritance
of this kingdom of magic and waste
recorded on camera, displayed,
entered in a little black notebook labelled
'Eduardo Paolozzi', a secret diary with cuttings
of newspaper peeping between leaves.
Essence is captured in scraps of wood,
fragments of cloth, a seed pod,
basketry, pottery, machinery, nuts and bolts,
cogs and wheels, ropes and braids, bulbs and beads,
the flotsam of humanity washes composite faces,
and the human hand engages to grab
while muted music plays on warrior pipes.

And as you leave, one line anonymous
comments on postcards may not go amiss.
Deposit them anywhere, your distilled emergences
for new audiences from east and west
to comment on your lost and found rapport,
like a vast undying conga flowing in and out
of this magic kingdom.

Note:
Eduardo Paolozzi (b. 1924) is a major 20th century sculptor and print-maker.
This poem was inspired by his 'Magic Kingdoms' exhibition in 1988.

Patrimony

'Demand your patrimony,' Mother said.
'Your father approaches. The moment's here!'
Her expression bitter, age lined her eyes.
Like destiny the crowd of monks grew near:
every hand held a beggar's bowl, every
head was shaved. She looked at, but did not see;
she could not, would not, point him out to me.

'A prince's first-born can ask anything
of his father. Some day you will be king.
Stake your claim. After long years he has come.'
I searched a saffron sea – each serene face.
The one with the confident stride drew me.

'I am called Rahul of the Sakya race.
Father, give me my due,' I insisted,
tugging hard at the lean monk's robe. 'Where
is my inheritance?' Mother's gaze now
was luminous, the stranger's full of care.

He handed me his empty bowl and looked
at her he'd left behind. He raised one hand
in showering blessing. 'Son, join our band,'
he said, begging forgiveness all the while.

His radiant face mirrored Mother's smile.

Notes
Rahul: son of the Buddha and Yashodara, at fifteen he followed his father's
example and joined the Sangha, the brotherhood of Buddhist monks.
Sakya: the Buddha's clan.

47

Sultana Razziya

I

'Sultana Razziya *zindabad*!'
The crowds shouted themselves hoarse
when none but you were left
between the throne and anarchy.

Long years ago, Iltutmish, your father,
had the wisdom-folly dictated
by desperation to name you his heir.
'We have always placed the sultanate
above all other interests,' he told
the silent surly noblemen. 'We did not
subdue Bengal, Bihar and Sind; crush
rebellions; avert the catastrophe
of Mongol hordes overrunning the land;
consolidate our empire; only
to have it all vanish like some desert
mirage in the next generation.'

'Sons were sons,' the durbar murmured.
But your sire knew all about ability.
Finger raised in admonition, he could
acknowledge the incompetence of sons:
'Remember Aram Shah, our brother-in-law,
great Qutb-ud-Din's disastrous progeny.
You yourselves begged us to bring an army
out of Baduan to rid you of this dynasty.
Our sons too are of that ruinous ilk.'

Only Iltutmish could have the audacity
and vision to name you a leader of men,
he likened your razor sharp mind to that
of blessed Ayesha. When a 'Slave of a Slave'
could occupy Delhi's peacock throne,

one could begin to contemplate
a mere daughter succeeding him.

All agreed, but when your father died, history
repeated itself – and your discretion lay
in waiting – it was Rukn-ud-Din Firoz
they raised and suffered, then deposed,
as your father's ghost watched him flounder
under the burdens of state. Chaos reigned,
till at last the mob cheered you heartfelt:
'Sultana Razziya *zindabad*!'

II

'Sultana Razziya *zindabad*!'
For the good of the many, in your father's name,
for the sake of the sultanate …
'She is her father's daughter!'
they praised. But what did that mean?
You knew that you were your own woman.

The crown adorned your curling locks,
crest of peacock feathers eyeing the multitude.
You did not want this, gently born,
what did you care for rule and power?
Yet leadership became you, you knew
where your duty lay, all your life you had
breathed the hot-house air of court intrigue.
You would grow into the job, you told yourself,
be the very model of a Muslim queen,
the flower of Indian womanhood.
When the court painter petitioned you
for sittings, you dispensed with the customary
lotus and rose, but posed in quarter profile,
your henna-patterned hands holding a drawn
sword – a delicious curve like Cupid's bow –
perhaps the artist saw beyond you.

You smiled at your cheering subjects,
promised them unity, protection, glory, peace.
The pillared halls echoed with lusty cries:
'Sultana Razziya *zindabad*!'

But almost at once the murmuring began:
'ruling a sultanate was no easy task
and women were ever frail, it was unnatural
to stay single at her age and the Sultana
needed the guidance of a man.'
Conspiracies were hatched, divisions emerged,
the powerful muscled their way to your presence,
bent on wedding power, power that lay with you.
But you were your own mistress now
and sent the sniffing wolfhounds packing,
though they waited at the gates, tongues lolling.

'We will not be ruled by a woman,' they said.
'Let us see how she copes in battle.'
Revolt spread like forest fires and each one
taxed you more than the last to stamp out.
You learnt to win some over with honeyed words,
others you had to fight, all had to be kept at bay.
Your glamorous figure riding with the troops
was hailed with shouts – and some unease:
'Sultana Razziya *zindabad*!'

III

But was this seemly, was this natural?
Every question returned to the basic one
of the rightness of a woman ruling alone
over civilized Muslim men. The Prime Minister
had much to say on the obscenity of your position.
His pastime was the writing of secret letters
and constant quoting from the Quran in conversation –
funny how often the subject was women!
Your duty lay in marriage, he said;

you should give the people what they were used to –
a sultan. But you were wilful.
Razziya, gently born, would have wed
some royal suitor at her father's bidding.
But Sultana Razziya would rule her own destiny.

By dint of ability, and with his master's example
beckoning, Iltutmish had risen from slave
to Governor to Sultan and, along the way,
had married the Sultan's daughter.
You, Sultana, favoured an Abyssinian slave.
When a man aspires, it is admired;
when a woman stoops, she is beneath forgiveness.

Open rebellion flared up: governors,
once your suitors, now waged war.
It could not last. No one was ready
for the phenomenon of a Muslim queen.
Though you paved the way for so many
Mughal wives to rule after you,
they did so from behind the purdah.
You led your soldiers into battle,
but they would not be led. Captured,
imprisoned, days numbered, you reflected on
the fickle kismet that led you here, to shouts of:
'Sultana Razziya *murdabad*!'

Notes
Sultana Razziya: talented daughter of Iltutmish, she ruled from 1236 to 1240 AD.
Zindabad! and *Murdabad*!: 'long live!' and 'death to!'
Iltutmish: Qutb-ud-Din Aibak's slave, he won his master's favour and was elevated
to Governor of Baduan. Later he replaced Qutb-ud-Din's son Aram Shah to
become sultan (1211-1236 AD). Since Qutb-ud-Din also rose from slave to
sultan, Iltutmish was called 'Slave of a Slave'. Although he appointed his daughter
Razziya to succeed him, two of his sons had brief spells as sultan: Rukn-ud-Din
Firoz after Iltutmish died and Nasir-ud-Din Mahmud a few years after Razziya
was put to death by her nobles.
Qutb-ud-Din: founder of the Slave Dynasty, he ruled the Delhi sultanate from
1206 to 1210 AD.
Ayesha: favourite wife of the Prophet Muhammad and a respected commentator
on the Quran and the Hadith.

Bhai Karim Afzal

Bhai Karim Afzal,
in childhood our worlds met:
we collected crickets and pigeon feathers,
I set my sights on music and song,
you spoke casually of medicine
being in your blood and bones.
One wall stood between us
and we played in courtyards under one sky.
We hopped back and forth between rooftops;
and the benign peepal tree,
demolishing garden boundaries,
was a passport to shared domains.
Today miles and years later,
we are India and Pakistan.

Bhai Karim Afzal,
nearest to that brother I never had,
I missed you when my family moved away.
When chance returned us to the old house again,
we were teenagers – tongue-tied.
Then I caught you one day in the garden:
absorbed,
knife bared –
blood – pain – twisted things
I recognised as frogs dissected,
more jars lined up
for the slaughter of experiment
in the secret corner where our friendship bloomed.
We gazed in an anguish of dismay
and rushed away in guilty sentiment.

Today miles and years later,
we are India and Pakistan.
You are a scientist in a provincial town

and I juggle between poetry and prose.
Between here and there, by chance
our different orbits met.
We were shy strangers,
loving regret between us.
Bhai Karim Afzal,
nearest to that brother I never had,
I miss you.

Notes
Bhai: 'brother' in several north Indian languages..
Karim: one of Allah's names, it is an Arabic word meaning 'merciful'.
Afzal: Urdu derivation from the Arabic 'Afdal', meaning 'the best', it is one of
Allah's names.
Peepal: a tree sacred to Hindus who will not cut it. Walls and buildings are
sometimes destroyed when it grows too near them.

Traffic

The traffic moves as traffic always does
– bar accidents.
We meet, we smile, we say 'hello'
– maybe.
Should we stop and for how long?
Shall we discuss the weather
or have we graduated from that
to higher or more intimate things?
How are you today?
I feel disposed to unbend a little
and tell you that you must visit us
– someday.
Are we ready to exchange confidences?
I hate those yellow shoelaces
– are you colour blind?

Did he pass by and incline his head?
Now what could that have meant?
Did her mouth curve upwards
and was there recognition in her eyes?
No, we did not hold each other
for more than a split second
– if that.

On a winter's day we walked by,
wrapped in fog and convention.
We each waited on the other
– except that we did not wait.
In a cool politeness that did nothing
to thaw the day,
relieved of the necessity
of acknowledgement,
cheated of the burden
of conversation,
vaguely dissatisfied,
we would not halt the traffic.
The traffic moves as traffic always does
– bar accidents.

Towers of Silence

When we were classmates, I told you my dreams, Homi:
dreams of Juliet against a London sky,
a matchmaking umbrella sheltering us,
even though it never rained in my dreams.
You clapped my back on Chowpatty beach
as we threaded our way through hawkers and pyedogs.
I was the one with an eye to the future,
but you always kept your head:
'Come to the pictures, *yaar*,' you'd say,
'and Aunty Mehroo's for a top class *chaat*.'

Campus life was an oasis that nourished
the branching of our separate ways.

Your letters are most solicitous; I sense
the happy marriage – product of careful planning
by family and friends, the steady grooming
of the business you partner with your uncle;
I picture the comfortable middle-aged spread,
not that the studio photograph shows it;
is your top balding, I wonder? Mine is.
You have landed on your feet.
I took off as I always knew I must –
I suppose I won some measure of success.
You ask about my dreams. In truth, Homi,
I don't remember them in the mornings.
But I know they are of home, for I awake each day
to the boisterous din of Bombay's traffic
raining echoes on a Docklands tenement.

Of course there are Parsees here. Past masters
at immigration, we know all about integration.
Our clubs are here and there. But back home
the towers of silence are calling me.

Notes
Yaar: pal
Chaat: a dish of spicy mixed fruit
Parsees: Zoroastrians descended from the Persians who fled to India from Muslim
persecution in the 7th and 8th centuries. Under the British Raj, Parsees took to
British education and adopted some British ways. They concentrated in Mumbai,
which developed into a great commercial centre. Parsees have excelled in
commerce, travelling to many business capitals around the world. Traditionally
they dispose of their dead by leaving them on their 'towers of silence'.

Fair Weather
(*an English-as-a-Foreign-Language poem*)

Hello friend! I am friendly, yes?
'Is fair weather'? Yes, very much:
sun is equal not-so-hot on all,
rain is ever on you, and me also ever,
cold is very much on all also.
English friend ever talk weather.
I come from sunshine very much –
I not like fair weather, so talk weather never.

Arrival

The cardinal winds have brought us here.
Now battered, now buoyant, we survived.
What mattered most was getting it clear:
no longer strangers, we have arrived.

From *A Little Bridge* (1997)

Snips and Snails
(For Freud's birth anniversary, 6ᵗʰ May 1996)

Iconoclast, you saw yourself:
      Moses breaking tablets.
Some saw a reluctant patron
      saint for surrealists –
      and how many others?
'Complete fools!' you damned them all

      till Dali shook your shell.
'That young Spaniard, with his candid
      fanatical eyes' absorbed
your gaunt octogenarian looks.
He raked into your mirrored gaze,
visioned your patriarchal head
      and drew it as – a snail!

You acknowledged the 'undeniable
      technical mastery',
but puzzled 'how he came to create
      that picture'. An analytical
investigation was in order.
Spiralled lines encased the brain.
      What totem was the snail?
What taboos surround its killing
      and its ritual eating?
No ordinary father, this:
little boy snips and snails drawn deep
      from the unconscious,
this shining trail you left behind.

      Bold dreamer, who saw who?
When the lean moustachioed figure
entered your dreams, while riding his own,
did you glimpse a larger hero
from your windmill-tilting youth,

basin jaunty on the head?
In exile, your days were numbered
but the immortal Spaniard struts,
forever wandering the world.
Don Sigmund, did you see yourself
in the Freudian knight of La Mancha?

Note
Quotations are from Earnest Jones' *The Life and Work of Sigmund Freud*
(Penguin Books, 1961).

Hungry Ghost

Today I went shopping with my father
after many years. I felt I was back
in time to when I'd follow grandfather
to the market, smelling the spicy scents,
drinking the sights and mingling with the shouts.
Neither buyer nor seller, I would float
like a restless spirit, hungry for life.

The market is bigger. I have grown too.
There are more goods as distances have shrunk.
The prices are higher. I understand
about money and, alas, its bondage
of buyers and sellers. Almost I wish
I was again that hungry ghost, watchful
and floating through the world's noisy bazaar.

Learning the Imperialist's Language

Because you were the enemy's,
you had to be grappled with
and ruthlessly mastered.
Encountering you was all
the delight of illicit romance.
Analysing you, I discovered
how the enemy thinks.
But this was not enough –
I looked for chinks in the armour;
you gave me the awful
lesson of linking with
what the enemy feels.

No more the enemy's,
you are now mine.
Even the bludgeoning
of rote-learning
brought us together.
You have schooled me
in strategies to disarm,
as you have fooled me
into owning at last,
that in possessing you,
I become the one-time enemy.

Words Between Us

Language breaks down and sounds have no meaning.
Words splutter, dialogues die in mid air;
you and I cross and there is no meeting.

Eyes do not glance, there is no encounter,
postures are hidden and gestures are bare;
language breaks down and sounds have no meaning.

Even masques expose the fading actor,
curtains are drawn but invite no fanfare.
You and I cross and there is no meeting.

We are less than strangers in theatre,
playing separate parts in solitaire.
Language breaks down and sounds have no meaning.

Silence replays the role of the jester.
No more are we one, no longer a pair.
You and I cross and there is no meeting.

Too many scenes have started to fester,
too many pauses are mimes that ensnare.
Language breaks down and sounds have no meaning.
You and I cross and there is no meeting.

Invitation to the Party

Now which party, friend, you are supporting?
My humble self am proclaiming always
the PPAF – People's Popular Action Front.
I am always in upfront with the Front. Ha ha!
Though I am only humble supporter,
but I know the leaps and bounds.

Always I am stickler in rules,
not like some *salés* who are always
defecating up private peoples' walls.
I am respecting of the people's property
and PPAF property more than all.
So when I see these Congresswallahs
have smudged everywhere their fat hands
and fingers also in cow-dung –
what holy waste I say –
and CPI *goondas* have propagated
the red weapon of propaganda,
in one-two Muslim districts also *haramzadas*
have misappropriated Lord Mahadev's crescent moon
and it is all upon slums in glorious inglory.
Ram Ram! I only spit always on all such places.
There are also elephants, parrots, lotuses –
now that is national flower and not for insult.
But you see, friend, how holy fauna flora
of Bharat is mass abused
on up and down walls. *Chhee chhee!*

Only yesterday I am telling
Nirmal's sister's nephew's friend,
our glorious Bharat has gone to dogs –
please to excuse this phoren expression.
What to do when talking phoren tongue
where even divine holiness God spelt from back
is something I cannot say
(always I am stickler in rules).
It is not like our own noble Sanskrit,
that is clean and heavenly
and most scientific even –
this all grey-mattered scientists are proving.
But *Haré Ram!* We don't live in Ram Raj now.
So phoren tongue is every tongues
more and more speedy with no respect for leaps and bounds
and phoren customs are corrupting young people.
This is only reason from last week

I am PPAF Founder member and President.
Responsibility is burdensome to humble self.
Now, friend, be sure you are voting
for back to Ram Raj and progress
for People's Popular Action Front.

Notes
Salés, *goondas* and *haramzadas* are all terms of abuse. Bharat is the Indian name
for India. Ram Raj or the 'reign of Rama' is considered a golden age.

Profound Thoughts of a Worldly Poet

Esteemed poet fellow and friend-to-be,
allow the pleasure to introduce you to myself.
I have only the recent happiness
to enrol in same poets' gathering
and am eager to embrace your distinguished feet
for training purposes. I am not for sitting
in garret and singing to myself.
My candle longs for union with the sun
which is glorious illumination
of all world poets. You may think I inhabit
a small town only, but I am worldly poet
in mind and heart, and patriot in politics.
You will be surprised to learn I am PPAF
Founder Member and Life President –
that is People's Popular Action Front –
and I endeavour to leave my mark on future
generation. This is why I invite
myself to local schools, turn by turn,
to give benefit of my profound thoughts
and poetry to innocent local children.
I am writing sonnets, ghazals, geets and odes

64

for many good years. Poetry beckons to me
like garland to bride. For example,
even this letter I am writing to you
is sheer poetry. I trust you will conserve it
and will kindly reply to me in kind.
Publishers do not take me seriously
because money has eaten them rotten
and they have no souls. Also ignorant
schoolteachers are calling themselves critics
and stabbing my poems in the back.
But I have hit on cunning methods
of getting at my public. My trips to schools,
free of charge, for noble inspiration
value, I have already explained.
But after enrolment in our same poets'
gathering, I requested membership list
like long roll of honour from Secretary.
With delight I see you abiding in Delhi,
P Lal in Calcutta, Nissim in Bombay,
Sujata in Germany, Keki in London,
and so on and ever onwards. How good to see
this spreading of our poetic genius.
Goddess Saraswati gave me idea
to write to each and every last and least
esteemed poet fellow and friend-to-be
with letter in poem form and extra poetry also.
So please to find in self-same envelope
two dozen more poems by humble self.
I will not do injustice of sending
one only for you cannot get all round
picture without shooting from every angles.
Blood and sweat and tears are in these poems,
so bloody good, I think. I eagerly wait
for your esteemed good opinions on everyone.
I will send detailed comments also on all
masterpiece poems you send to me,
so it is tit for tat and this is that!

Please be forthcoming with names and addresses
of your publishers, local schools and colleges
and all your friends for getting at wider circle in your name.
I remain your humble *chela* in poetry
and also PPAF Founder Member
and, not to mention, first and Life President.

P.S. PPAF enrolment form
is enclosed. Five rupees discount to all
esteemed poet fellows and friends-to-be.

Notes
Saraswati is the Goddess of Learning and the Arts. *Chela* means 'disciple'.

A Square of the Raj
(*For Renee D'Arcy Haigh*)

In Ranchi two cemeteries lie side by side,
silent above the steamy plains.

The Christian cemetery, still in use,
has gone native and unkempt;
wild weeds straggle expansive
in a blasphemy of tall grass.
There is no thought of keeping up
with the departed Jones's over the wall
whose military plot orders a square
of the Raj, meticulous forever:
a puny foothold in the wilderness.
Tombstones stand in midget uniform size,
rows of English pocket handkerchief lawns
spread green in front, only kneeling space
to read the carved names on stone.

My husband and I come on a personal mission,
a family matter, an attempt at human meeting.
Like ghosts we glide in the soundless air.
1533197 CORPORAL
W D'ARCY
ROYAL AIR FORCE
30 MAY 1945 AGE 38
reads a tablet, under RAF wings
and with a cross below;
clean cut as on every stone of every
husband, brother, father, son.
Does he seem closer now, I wonder,
to the man who grips my brown hand?
Do all here sense our presence?
With flowers and Ganges water
I salute my father-in-law,
bid him and his comrades rest.

Three gardeners in sepoy khaki,
government-appointed, water and tend
the graves of strangers who shed
their bodies so far from home
in a fading bugle cry of empire.
They rush to don cloth caps and shoes
to be photographed at attention,
teeth flashing, by the obligatory memorial,
proud of their handiwork
this side of the wall.

Not Your Average Snake

I'm not your average snake in the grass,
I don't slither shiver any old spine.
    I am the speckled band
    that ornaments the hand,
delicately dispensing decisions
of life and death by Manasa Devi.

I'm not your apple-tempting sneak serpent.
I don't seduce those innocent of shame.
    I am the quick thinking,
    quivering, day-saving,
prayer-knot round Ganesha's pot belly,
holding contentment, jam-packed and spilling.

I'm not the viper battering Heaven,
injecting venom with my fruity words.
    I am the effortless,
    cooling, clinging, necklace,
twined to comfort Shiva's blue martyred throat.
We are twin kings, dancing in ecstasy.

I'm not the fanged beast reigning over Hell,
striking fear with forked and flickering tongue.
    I am the tireless rope;
    my turning is the hope
of gods and demons churning the ocean.
I, Vasuki, raise order from chaos.

Notes
Manasa Devi is the Hindu Snake Goddess, Ganesa is the Elephant-headed God
of Wisdom, and Vasuki was a giant serpent used by the gods and demons to
churn the ocean at the beginning of creation and gather its treasures. Vasuki's
venom was swallowed by the Destroyer God, Shiva, turning his throat blue.
Shiva is also called Neelkantha ('blue-throated') and Nataraja ('King of Dance').

Satguru

Five rivers bathe your feet,
Nanak of Talwandi.

The four directions bow
in praise of He who is
in each place that you turn.

For three days Sulakhni
searched for her husband gone,
but you had found your goal.

Two precious sons were born
to you, but the wide world
became your family.

You had answered the call
of One beyond compare.

Mardana at your side,
you sing His countless names.

Householder, ascetic,
not Hindu, not Muslim,
true Guru serving all.

Five rivers bathe your feet,
Nanak of Talwandi.

Notes
Satguru means 'true guru'.
Talwaandi: Guru Nanak's birthplace in the Punjab – 'the land of the five
rivers'. Sulakhni: Guru Nanak's wife.
Mardana: a Muslim musician-disciple of Guru Nanak.

Visiting E M Forster

"But Forster doesn't live here any more."
I knew that of course. He died the year before
– before my passage. I told 'Raised Eyebrows'
that I only wanted ... to see his room,
to see the view. Why else would I have come?
"But this is not a museum, you know."
(Cambridge, not a museum?) I nodded.
"An ordinary room." Ordinary
is what it takes. I remembered my coach
journey from Canterbury. "I have come
all the way from India. He was my friend."
It worked. The brows subsided, defeated.

A bemused stranger occupied the place
– half apologised for everything changed.
The room was functional, anonymous:
he could not have lived here long. "I'm afraid
even the furniture is not the same."
What did I care, standing at the window.
Olive groves beside the forget-me-not
Mediterranean rolled below, with
a dust haze veiling the Marabar curves.
"It is the same," I said, "nothing has changed."

From *Albino Gecko* (1998)

Albino Gecko

Uncommon gecko, wraith on the ceiling,
dream-dinosaur descendent,
clinging to the world – upside down,
soft-padding across the lime-washed surface,
gliding from behind the photograph
of my grandparents' Guru,
monitor of my homework hours.

'Gecko, gecko, on the wall,
are you the smartest swot of all?'

Studies stretch my fluorescent evenings
on the rack, in partnership
with your patient seconds and timeless minutes
of immobility –
all comes to those who wait.
Only your darting and striking punctuate
the pinioned stillness and relieve the air.

'Gecko, gecko, on the wall,
are you the wisest fool of all?'

I feel inflated at the flight insects
dispatched into the great unknown
of your transparent depths.
I feel elated at your acrobatics,
your yoga fascinates.
You grin, wide-mouthed, at gravity,
swivel a heavy lidded eye
and flick your flexible tail at death.

'Gecko, gecko, on the wall,
are you the deadliest clown of all?'

'What happens if a gecko falls
on your head?' My scalp crawls.
Does a gecko, so sure-footed, ever fall?
'You will be a raja if it falls
on your head by accident.'
Can one contrive an act of nature?
There's magic in these old wives' tales
from monsoon nights of an age gone by.

'Gecko, gecko, on the wall,
are you the greatest king of all?'

Monitor of my homework hours,
uncommon gecko, wraith on the ceiling,
holding back the hordes of tyranny:
mosquitoes, moths and millions
of fluttering mindless wings
that try to rule my childhood prison
and drain away my youth.

'Albino spectre on the wall,
you are the strangest ghost of all.'

From Silence

"Speech is… but silence is golden."
"Little girls should be seen, not heard."
What bully shut our silver mouths?
 ("In the beginning was the Word.")

Silence is ripening yearning,
listening. Let my silence grow –
silence to nurture thoughtful speech.
From silence may my language flow.

The Geisha

Gliding soft on *tatami* mats,
she was silent, invisible,
like a paper screen pulled across.
Yet the blank room had a precise
ikebana that bore her touch.
Her laugh was an apology,
hidden by a delicate fan;
her eyes were careful to avoid
stares at her butterfly beauty.
Ordered teatimes saw her preside
with a quiet formality.
Each morning she removed the beds
and effaced herself from the day.

Notes
tatami: straw matting used on Japanese floors.
ikebana: Japanese art of flower arrangement.

Seasons

Dandelions clock
   in the season's racing sun;
      yellows blanche in time.

Koinobori

Once again at Koinobori, the fish
have leapt from pools and rivers to conquer
our land and sky. An army of colour,
flying assorted banners, they come in
all sizes and rich shapes, drawn from the sea.
Fins and tails that slice the waves, now propel
the enchanted air, gills breathe and scales sing.
Japan is festooned, its children delight
while fish follow them as they run and play.
They quiver and shimmer to shout and leaps.
There are more than koi carp and mackerel;
fantasy creatures become familiar.
Lives streak with a moment's iridescence.

Note
Koinobori: carp streamers called koinobori are flown from Japanese homes
from mid April to mid May in honour of Children's Day on May 5.

Bamboo

Bamboo notches gird
green saplings, dark kimono
sashes at the waist.

The breeze flutters leaves,
a geisha's coded promise
patterned in her fan.

Trees are storm-black strokes,
calligraphy adorning
the sky's rain-washed page.

There is Method to my Madness

You too are one of those
who always count their toes
    and stand and stare.
    Beware! Beware!
        Am I mad today?
    Why should you care?
        Somewhat sane, let's say.
There is method to my madness.

You ask me how I feel:
my skin is orange peel.
    With tooth and claw
    you probe a raw
        luminous jelly within
    and gape in awe.
        Guilty questions fret my sin.
There is method to my madness.

A clever stupid smile
still glitters in exile.
    Can't hear my screams?
    Blood flows in streams.
        Bastard, why must I explain?
    The air throbs dreams;
        don't you also feel the pain?
There is method to my madness.

I dare not try to speak,
perhaps these walls know Greek.
    Your tape records the silence.
    The truth lies masked by pretence
        because I can't be bothered
    to dredge my words from immense
        caves where we all lie smothered.
There is method to my madness.

When the Telegram Came
(for Brian)

You'd never open my mail,
a 'principle' with you
– one that makes no sense
to me in marriage;
your English otherness.

You must have practised not opening
till it was second nature.
I was often away and would ask you
to determine their urgency.
'Oh no!' you'd say, 'nothing
is so urgent that it can't wait
a few days' – privacy
was sacred. Were we not two
who made a greater one?
But you valued my separate
wholeness – and besides
my mail was mostly junk!

Then the telegram came
– we were expecting it
sooner or later,
or something like it from India.
Time was no factor
in anticipating
or measuring the blow.
You slit it open
– you wished to spare me
its wrenching opening.

You rang me at work
– your voice, as always, mellow.
The tone said something,
your silence something more.

I asked only twice
and you spared me
the unknowing knowing.

Did I want to come home?
Should you come to fetch me?
'No, I want to walk,' I said.
Single-mindedly
I wanted my sister back.

I left early. 'Just check
the shutters, Sheena, when you leave.'
Such madness in routine!
The sky so smoothly blue,
the January breeze so crisply fresh
– was this same sky above my parents too?
What air did my sister's children breathe?
Thrusting green and steel surrounded me.
I felt both alive and dead
as I crept uphill,
looking down on the calm
of a city on another planet.
Where was the relief
of the celebrated British weather?

I thought of you waiting
and the sister you lost
many years before we met.
Why couldn't I have known her
and been there for you?
It was a time for human questions
and childish railing.
I went home to you.

Parrot Feathers

Letters held all we had between us,
they were everything.
They were our youth, beauty, even truth –
and parrot feathers coloured our lives.
So when they dwindled
                                    and stopped –
as my intended one
                                    became another's –
so many letters between us stayed unwritten
to prop up the world.

Then you came once more in fading light,
but it was a tryst
                                    with a difference.
My intended one
                                    would be another's bride.
You bit your lip as you asked
for their return.
You might as well have begged me
to roll back the tide.
Mine, you said, were already burnt,
but I read the lie in those bright eyes.
'Not the feathers?' I whispered,
and you turned away.

I gave away the precious bundle
that housed, but did not contain,
your words choreographed in my memory.
These I cannot return,
or the many unwritten letters you sent,
nor the many more that will continue
to fill the emptiness.
Letters hold all we have between us.

Note
The parrot is sacred to Kama, the Hindu God of Love.

The Age of Kalkin

Even prayers die in the twilight
of the Bhishmas of Kurukshetra.
Bharat's children continue to fight
though desperate times bring no Krishna,
the Yadavas died out and Dwarka
crumbles beneath the turbulent sea.

No monkey army builds the Babri.
Madness stalks the wastes of Ayodhya,
while golden temples ring grim fury.
This land holds no welcome for Rama.
Hindus, Muslims, Sikhs, tear India.
Kalkin Avatar murders the light.

Notes
Kalkin: the last avatar whose coming will mean the end of the world.
Krishna of the Yadava clan was born at Ayodhya and ruled over Dwarka in
western India. He promised that the avatar will always appear when needed to
deliver the righteous and to punish evil-doers.
Rama was another avatar of Vishnu who was helped by monkeys to build a
bridge across the ocean.
Bhishma: a venerable hero who died on the battlefield of Kurukshetra in *The
Mahabharata*.

Dancing Ganapati

Dancing Ganapati, trunk in the air,
we loved you and fed you on milk and sweets,
smeared sandal paste on your marble brow,
decked your pachyderm neck with fresh marigold,
beat on our drums and danced while you stared
with ears fanned out, for we hailed you in joy.
We waved oil lamps and swayed as we sang:
'Dancing Ganapati, trunk in the air,
bless us who worship with milk and sweets.'

We slipped away, ate and drank in your name.
Life was as always: flesh-stoned together,
you were our friend, we knew where you stood.
Dancing Ganapati, trunk in the air,
we drank your milk and savoured your sweets
till the day you chose to take our treats –
we wondered where all the milk had gone,
and stared in disbelief at our old playmate:
dancing Ganapati, trunk in the milk!

No Chrysalis

Fragile wings testing the air,
we are born beautiful.
But we grow larvaed layers
that harden.

People are not like butterflies.

An Indian Drink in Time
(From Foreign Service Circular, 1969)

Alcoholic drinks are to be avoided.
Embassy personnel should be mindful
that prohibition is in place
in the Motherland
and the homes of our diplomats
are mini Indias abroad.
At parties, the serving
of *nimbu-pani* cocktails
is to be encouraged.
This is of course refreshing
and a distinctly
Indian drink
that will go down well.

(From Foreign Service Circular, 1972)

All diplomats abroad are urged
to take a pride in Indian goods.
Swadeshi won us independence.
Our export products
are a high standard and win
much needed foreign exchange.
Promote them at social functions.
At all embassy cocktails
delight the guests
with Indian whisky.

Notes
nimbu-pani: 'lemon-water'
Swadeshi: 'one's own country', a nationalist movement in India.

Sacred Cow

Gods and demons fought over you,
Kamadhenu, cow of plenty.
Treasure from the ocean's churning,
you are the gentle Earth's best form:
patience, mercy, serenity.

You chose us. Our screaming hungers
drew you. You gave yourself freely –
India, Egypt, Mother Earth –
always undemanding Nature,
cud-chewing roadside deity,
familiar, taken for granted.

Great Brahma honours you and loves
the Earth whose pure eyes shine in you.
You were a measure of the wealth
and power of kings; you measure
now the humanity of man.

You who gift us milk, tears, silence,
know our warring gods and demons.
siphon our greed and violence.
Casually worshipped, guardian
of stray street corners, your strong tail
is our lifeline to other shores.

Notes
Kamadhenu: In Hindu mythology, Kamadhenu the wish-fulfilling cow was one
of the prizes discovered by the gods and the demons in their churning of the
ocean.
The ancient Egyptians also worshipped a heavenly cow, Hathor. Bhoomi Devi
the Earth Goddess assumes the form of a cow when she appears to Brahma the
Creator to complain about her sufferings. In Hindu tradition, even a wicked
person is assured of salvation if holding on to a cow's tail at the moment of death.

Lakshmana's Regret

She could have taught humility
itself the meaning of 'humble';
but I was too proud to accept
her simple devotion – I was not my brother.

She was like the wild Jujube tree
growing outside her hut –
scraggly, small and thin,
with grey bark cracked,
but O she was evergreen!

Praise the Mother, that one of us brothers
could be a loving son,
for I saw only a wrinkled hag
who delayed us with opportuning.

I marked Elder Brother's reverence
and bowed in silent reverie.
I never had his ease with women,
young or old. Demoness, goddess,
princess or beggar – I armoured myself
against their sorcery. I was not my brother.

He sat down to bask in her love,
for all the world as if Sita did not weep
and Ravana did not wait for his nemesis.

My baffling brother stretched a greedy palm
in which old Shabari placed her berries
like so many sugar-plums – all her worldly wealth,
each fruit bitten and sweetness-tested
for offering to her princely guests.

Elder Brother relished those berries
but my finicky delicacy

made me throw away my share
with a careless discretion.
I was not my brother.

Later he said that Shabari was a celestial –
and Elder Brother never lied.
I forgot the incident until

many moons later when I died.

My head on Brother's lap, the juice
of divine Sanjivani was squeezed into my mouth,
and I revived to be told
that the life-giving herb had grown
from those berries carelessly sown.

Note:
Lakshmana is Rama's loyal younger brother in *The Ramayana*. On the way to
rescue Sita from the demon Ravana, they encounter Shabari. Rama's blessing
releases Shabari from a curse so that she can return to Heaven. The epic tells this
story, as well as the one in which the Sanjivani herb restores Lakshmana to life.

Nobody's Cat

Her bio-data says she lived alone
with her lover, two lap-dogs and a bird.

Neighbours sometimes smiled. But her plight remained.

She could have added the plant and goldfish,
even the divan, Georgian fireplace
and Picasso reproduction. Maybe
she collected them all, but they belonged.

She moved, odd one out, like nobody's cat.

Across the Black Waters

Turn your thoughts to the deeds of those
disciples of both sexes
who offered their heads
for the sake of their faith,
were cut to pieces,
...offered sacrifices in performing services in Gurdwaras,
did not lose their faith,
kept long hair till their
last breath, O Khalsa!
Utter Wahiguru!
(from Guru Gobind Singh's "Ode to God", *Ardas*, translated by
Sangat Singh)

It's fifty years since the old man unpacked the War.
It spilled out from the battered army holdall
which now lives in the attic of our terraced house.
"Subedar Surjeet Singh" has all but faded
from the grimy olive green.

He had given an eye for the king-emperor
and wore a patch with pride.
We long since gave up talk of glass substitutes,
for it would start him counting lives.
"Our village sacrificed every mother's son,
our bravest lions," he'd shake his turbaned head.
"A single eye is a small price for victory.
Didn't Ramchandra pluck his lotus eye
in offering before he battled demons?"
Then he'd chuckle as he remembered other heroes:
Lord Nelson and Ranjit Singh. He loved it
when Mother called him the one-eyed Maharaja.
He spoke of the great man as of a saviour.

"*Sab lal ho jayega*, all will be red!"
He read much into those prophetic words:

"And Hindustan was red with the Raj's red sepoys,
and *Vilayat* across the black waters reddened with our blood."
His one eye would glisten for comrades lost
and his voice trailed into the mountains and plains
of North Africa and Southern Italy...

When we were kids with knotted hankies on our heads,
Mother told of how the old man trudged the Yorkshire streets
with his starched turban and military step, his fierce eye
quelling the stone-throwing urchins who called him "Gypsy".
"No dogs, no niggers, no Irish," said the pinched landladies,
but his card tricks would sometimes earn a cup of tea.

Recently my son said we should put him in a home –
I'd have hit him if he'd been younger.
I told him how the old man had fought in the War,
and how afterwards he'd sold coloured silks from door to door
till he could buy a market stall.

But sometimes I wonder myself.
The old man doesn't leave the attic now.
There he waters his fields in the Indian sun
and communes with the Khalsa.
All his English has gone, except "left-right-left"
endlessly as he marches at all hours of the night.
At three in the morning I complained that his stamping
kept us awake; I had work in the morning, the youngest
was sitting 'A' levels. But he laughed.
It was morning in India and the buffaloes needed milking!

Sometimes I think of sending him back,
but there's nowhere left.
His village isn't even in India now.
The land of five rivers exists only in his memory.

My son, a computer analyst, speaks no Punjabi
and will never understand. How could he?

The old man doesn't recognise him, yet
he knows the names of long-dead regimental friends!

What can I say? I too remember the day
I returned from University –
clean-shaven, de-turbaned –
and the shock of betrayal in the old man's eye.
"Papaji, I want a decent job," I pleaded.
"It was you who wanted me to be an engineer,
you who said we have to fit in."
"The army took us," he muttered. "We ate the *Sarkar's* salt."
He wouldn't look at me for several days, but stared
at his youthful photo-self: neat black beard rolled up
and thick moustache pointing up to a proud khaki turban.
It was Mother who made him face me again:
"Maharaja Ranjit Singh would have forgiven," she said.

But Mother and the Maharaja are dead, and the old man
is only a one-eyed illiterate peasant from a divided land.

Notes
Wahiguru: 'wonderful Lord', a term used frequently by Sikhs in the course of
worship.
Khalsa: the Sikh brotherhood, founded by Guru Gobind Singh in 1699. Men and
women are admitted to the Khalsa at an initiation ceremony.
Ramchandra: hero of *The Ramayana*. He offered one of his eyes to the Goddess
Durga as a substitute for a lotus.
The one-eyed Maharaja, Ranjit Singh (1780-1839), was a great Sikh hero.
Vilayat: 'the West'.
Sarkar: 'Government'.

From the Base

Easy to succumb to Kali Yuga:
relive our nightmares, accepting defeat;
but this is not the way to scale the heights.

Action – collective or single – creates.
Give no dumb assent to self-destruction,
we are our own avatars in this age.

Time's cyclic wheel is not the enemy
when our breath can turn it anti-clockwise.
Drawn stick-figures, we have fleshed beyond the frame.

Reflection shapes us, our feelings flower;
we raise questions, regardless of answers:
what crowns the summit is not our concern.

Born at the base, our eyes must search upwards,
our natural response – to step forward.

Note
Kali Yuga: the Dark Age that precedes the final destruction of this world cycle.

Manu's Wife

Manu was the first man.
And I?
        I too was there.

I noticed his unilateral decision
To confer his name on mankind.

90

'Man in the general
Embraces woman,' he said.

He was never strong
On logic and envied me.

I let him lean his death-fear on me.
He needed to be remembered.

His inability to create
Made him codify and list rules.

He spent much time defining
My place in his world.

I needed no analysis
To discover our difference.

When he proposed, he boasted
He was Brahma's mind-born son.

No womb begat him.
It explains a lot!

He thought me impressed
Enough to wed him.

But I was woman in the raw;
Subversive. I would survive him.

And Manu was the only other.
And I?
            I was there, laughing.

Note
Manu: the progenitor of the human race and the primal man who
codified laws for Hindu society.

Romance, Bollywood Style

Rain-drenched sari silhouetted against
the Victoria Memorial's white,
she warbles at him flying a pink kite:
romance behind inevitable trees.

– Except that stretching flat from that façade
of empire is only a parched maidan
where the teeming millions 'promenade'.
No tree in sight, but the Ochterlony
Monument jutting upstart at one end,
like a Brahmin's head with cheeky choti.

From the summit of the Kutb Minar
her *dupatta* floats down like a trophy
caught by the hero smoking Charminar
cigarettes on the ground and her lips mime
a love ditty. Across coy distances
spring teasing promises in clichéd rhyme.

– Except that suicide leaps by unknowns
craving a moment's fame in death, have meant
that tourists are prevented from ascent
to any heights that may be danger-prone.

Coiffured picture on a postcard mountain,
she skis across glaciers. *The hoi polloi*
in movie halls gape at her bikini.
She yodels a duet with lover boy
who plays a bagpipe, sitting miles away
on a houseboat on Dal Lake, lamenting
the loss of Radha. Ah, Krishna, is this
your legacy of tricks? Your flute and play?

Prancing pink against the marbled coolness
of the Taj, hysterically giddy

in the midst of a fountain, she splashes
water at companions in comedy,
like some mad mahout, desperate to bathe
his pets, though they've trumpets for showering!

– And why be amazed that there's no tourist
in sight? Have India's millions vanished?
They are everywhere, eyes glued to the scene
cast in bright Technicolor on the screen.

Mumtaz Mahal and Shah Jahan lie tombed,
but Kama and Kubera save us from
their successors in Hindi cinema,
for: Heer and Ranjha, Laila and Majnun,
Nala and Damayanti, and Shakuntala
and Dushyanta, are the stuff of legends
and were never like this.

Notes

maidan: Anglo-Indian word for an open space in town or a parade-ground.
choti: pigtail.
dupatta: a long scarf worn by women.
Kama and Kubera: Hindu gods of Love and Wealth. The other characters in the poem are celebrated lovers from history and Punjabi, Arabic and Sanskrit Literatures.

Writing to Comfort Nehru's Daughter

Hindi did not come easy,
a hard and hybrid alien.
It was not her mother tongue.

So it was the national
language. Nothing to do with
quality or richness, but
everything with politics.

No sweet reverberations
of so much Indian speech.
Where was the dry brilliance
of English scattered like dust?

Even Chacha Nehru lent
such grace to the medium
which gave insight to *Glimpses*,
access to *Discovery*.

She laboured, disgusted through
extra coaching, oppressive
essay assignments, Kabir's
dohas duly memorized
without study, alphabets
daily butchered in orgy.

Then Nehru's tryst with death. Schools
and colleges closed. No time
for heated language riots.
Grief communicates itself,
though tortuous its channel.

She set herself the task of
writing to comfort Nehru's

daughter in *rashtra bhasha*.
Childish, but panascopic,
Hindi did not come easy,
a hard and hybrid alien.

Notes
Chacha: 'Uncle'.
Glimpses and *Discovery*: Nehru's books: *Glimpses of World History*, written
from prison as letters to his daughter, and *Discovery of India*, are classics of
Indo-Anglian Literature.
Kabir's *dohas*: Kabir (1440-1518) was a North Indian saint whose mystical
teaching attracted both Hindu and Muslim followers. He composed many popular
dohas or 'prayers'.
rashtra bhasha: 'national language'.

Ganga's Son

I

Can I curse the curse that made me
a refugee?
It was the cost
of Heaven lost.
Santanu mourned each drowning son
my waters won
more than his throne
could ever own.
But what of you, our eighth-born prince?
The king has since
broken his vow.
I am home now.

II

Bhishma, Heaven can only mean
a home unseen
and your mother
is the river
you walk beside when seized by doubt.
You are devout
and your royal
love is loyal
beyond the king's understanding.
His second Spring
banks on your vow,
King-maker now.

III

Watched from both river and sky,
you will not die
like other men.
You may choose when
you have endured enough of life.
Yet human strife
seduces you
to play Vishnu:
knock heads together and save the world.
But Krishna's hurled
into this age –
Son, turn your page.

Note:
Cursed by Brahma to spend time on Earth as King Santanu's wife, Ganga (the
Ganges) gave Santanu a condition: he must never question her actions. But,
seeing her drown seven sons in succession, the king had to question her when he
saw her take their eighth son to the river. Released from her curse, Ganga returned
to Heaven where her seven sons – really seven sages who had been similarly
cursed – had already gone. Bhishma, the heroic eighth prince, helped his father
to remarry by renouncing his own claim to the throne and taking a vow of celibacy.

Fifty Years Late

In the year of *Swaraj*, nineteen hundred
and forty-seven, millions were sent
card invitations in the people's name:
"Come friends and comrades, you are honoured guests,
come to the *mela* of independence.
Feast on freedom's fruits and cast off your chains,
welcome to democracy's jamboree."

The cards were smart, they were tricolour bright
and embossed with Ashoka's lion pride.
"RSVP" they said, but there was no response.

Some fell by the way, lost in freedom's post.
Some never reached the homeless whose address
was simply "India". Some were returned:
"Address unknown" or even "Redirect"
hopefully to a non-existent Raj.

The cards were smart, they were tricolour bright
and embossed with Ashoka's lion pride.
"RSVP" they said, but there was no response.

Some of the cards almost reached, but the guests,
they were too busy, so very busy.
Some fasted and prayed, others licked their wounds,
"Do not disturb for one generation"
notices nailed on doors, so embarrassed
invitations silently passed them by.
Some wailed and mourned their ancient nation-state:
"Our two eyes are plucked out to East and West,
how shall we see the doves of peace?" they wept.
"Our torn limbs are scattered to East and West,
we may not even beat our breasts and O
our families are gone!
My brother is killed, my daughter is raped,

I am buried alive.
So freedom's song is a slap on the face,
democracy's dance is a *tandava*
dance, devouring all in its dreadful wake."

The cards were smart, they were tricolour bright
and embossed with Ashoka's lion pride.
"RSVP" they said, but there was no response.

The guests were busy, so very busy.
They were napping, dreaming, snoring, gobbling
chaat, chewing *masala* and *paan*,
admiring the envelope, discussing
the wording and symbols, writing theses,
arguing about all the invitees.
"Who was a guest?" they asked, "and who a host?"
Their cards gathered dust on the mantelpiece.

The cards were smart, they were tricolour bright
and embossed with Ashoka's lion pride.
"RSVP" they said, but there was no response.

The guests multiplied and the cards grew scarce.
Collectors' items, some graced museums –
"pre-paper re-cycling sample" read the label –
and exchanged hands on the black-market.
Some were retrieved from under the mats.
"The time has come," some said, "to be merry.
Let's feast at freedom and democracy."
In the capitalist nineteen hundred
and ninety-seven, millions turned up,
dog-eared cards in hand.
'Midnight's Children' were knocking at the gate.
The guests had arrived fifty years late.

The cards were dull, the tricolour faded
and Ashoka's lion was flattened out.
"RSVP" was obliterated.

The hosts were busy, so very busy.
They were napping, dreaming, snoring, gobbling
chaat, chewing *masala* and *paan*.
"Who was a host?" they asked, "and who a guest?"

The guests keep clamouring: "We're the people,
'Midnight's Children' determined to party.

Our cards are smart, they are tricolour bright
and embossed with Ashoka's lion pride.
'RSVP' they say, and we're here to respond."

Notes
Swaraj: independence.
mela: fair.
Ashoka: a great Buddhist emperor (269-232AD) in India.
tandava: Shiva's cosmic dance which will destroy the world and start a new
cycle of creation.
chaat: spicy mixed fruit dish.
masala: condiments.
paan: betel leaf usually chewed after a meal.

Other Shores

In the joy of birdsong I forget to pick the flowers;
Their distant music sweeps me to other shores, other hours.

So now I arrive with an empty basket to your door.
The worship hour is gone; shame fixes my glance to the floor.

Your lamps and incense sticks are burnt, your priests are asleep.
Fading perfumes haunt my guilt – my blooms and prayers must
keep.

But Lord of my life, you laugh and draw me inside your door.
Your cupped hands dip into my basket, drawing birdsong and more.

My heart is full for you have filled me with worship's flowers:
Every bird-note is woven into garlands and bowers.

Your lamps and incense sticks are lit again and I remain
Singing, dancing. Immortal your name, your glory my gain.

Square Peg

I was a knight of the Round Table –
I killed dragons for my livelihood.

I was offered voluntary redundancy
for today's dragons have all been given knighthoods.

Jumbo Haiku Proverbs

In the elephant
orchestra, don't expect to
blow your own trumpet.

If you belittle
the elephant, prepare for
jumbo to squash you.

Atalanta's Game

He thought he caught me
by throwing golden apples.
I let him – and won.

Proverbial Logic

Where there are pandas
there's bamboo, but the converse
is sadly not true.

All Whom I Welcome Leave Without my Leave

All whom I welcome leave without my leave,
Just as they come without invitation.
I am not their host, so why do I grieve?

Respite from sickness is a mere reprieve,
Death remains the final registration.
All whom I welcome leave without my leave.

While greying hair and shades of old age cleave
To me, those I love abandon station.
I am not their host, so why do I grieve?

Because I wear my heart upon my sleeve,
I stumble, prey to Death's revelation:
All whom I welcome leave without my leave.

A spectator's role I cannot achieve;
My life explodes in participation.
Though I am not their host, must I still grieve?

I writhe in every net that Fate may weave.
Wisdom accepts my human condition.
All whom I welcome leave without my leave;
I am not their host, so why do I grieve?

From *Jade Horse Torso* (2003)

Jade Horse Torso

Han dynasty horse
of dappled aquamarine,
survivor of long centuries
in cool jade segments,
gleaming torso twisting
through cabinet glass,
stone nostrils flared
to test the gallery air,
ears peaked and pointing in
above a glistening brow
and chiselled eyes.

        The clean-cut mane is chipped,
        your broad chest muscle-tensed,
        your firm mouth open to neigh
        a triumphant challenge down
        your sea-horse-elongated nose,
        your noble head ready to soar
        as you rear on absent legs,
        your potent quarters vanished
        in a Chinese whisper,
        and dragon wings perhaps
        or coiled sea creature's tail…

        Precious horse from a green past,
        astride you, we ride beyond
        our jaded present
        into waves of foam-flecked
        dappled dreams.

Watching the Male Mute

(a 'found poem' on reading *Birdwatching
on Inland Fresh Waters* by M A Ogilvie)

The resident and very tame Mute Swan
adopts a firm line with his offspring.

Few birds are more aggressive
in defence of their young,
neck feathers flared in furious display,
charging red-eyed over the water with wings
outstretched, feet flapping the surface,
soundly slapping the elements.

Late autumn – all this changes.

On lake or gravel pit
the male Mute may be seen
defending territory
against all comers.
The cygnets too are now intruders.
He vigorously chases
until they are driven well away.
Singly or together,
despatch them he will.

Such parental aggression can cause
some spectators a certain measure of distress:
it does rather seem as if he is striving
to kill his own young just days
after safeguarding them.
But it is a natural part of the swan's life.

The Mute Swan's method of sending
offspring out into the wide world
appears to work.

Enterprising Harmony
(*a Star Trek ghazal*)

Science Officer, Mr Spock, raises pointed hand and brow,
and in his usual fashion says: "Live long and prosper."

I am James T Kirk, Star Trek Captain of the Enterprise;
united, my universal crew live long and prosper.

But Mr Spock is always showing off, upstaging me.
The last thing I want for him is to live long and prosper.

He's a pointy-eared Vulcan imp while I'm only human,
and drama needs conflict – so we can't live long and prosper.

On the other hand, our ratings call for happy endings;
so, for better or worse, Spock and Kirk live long and prosper.

Star Trek Epitaph

Here lies Captain Kirk of the Enterprise,
Beamed up by Death to the final frontier.
Boldly gone where many have gone before,
Kirk and crew enjoy one last adventure.

Five Things to do in Waiting Room
to Get You Noticed

Just nip out to the corridor and, in a twirl or two
   – a ballerina pirouette of course – change your costume
and go save the world. Then return to your place in the queue.
   Super heroes set good examples in the waiting room.

While others check out the magazines or attempt crosswords,
   flip out that *War and Peace* you carry around to impress
on these occasions. Insert a page-mark about two-thirds
   of the way. Soon you will feel flushed with the rush of success.

Do a spot of yoga meditation – nothing tranquil –
   I'm talking headstands, bellows-breathing and breath retention.
The lion pose – rolling eyes and tongue well out – will fulfil
   your objective of capturing everyone's attention.

Read: 'Five Things to do in Waiting Rooms to Get you Noticed'
   and respond without inhibition. Either read aloud
for ALL to hear, assume they are deaf and need your practised
   and boisterous laughter. Therapy – that; infects a crowd.

Or at the very least, jot down your 'Five Things *Not* to do'.
   It may give you perverse pleasure, but won't provide much
                             wealth.
Or waggle your ears and twiddle your thumbs – that's restful too.
   No one can say that you neglect your own or others' health!

Bahadur Shah Zafar
(*For Basir Sultan Kazmi*)

But two yards of land were all you wanted.
Your blind eyes shed tears for your motherland,
Every inch of her soil was sacred.

"Hindustan's last emperor," they taunted,
"Where are they now, the Mughals – great and grand?"
But two yards of land were all you wanted.

The slaughter of your princes was flaunted,
Martyred blood flooded the Yamuna's sand.
Every inch of her soil was sacred.

Dead eyes gazed from Delhi gates, tormented.
History has noted their desperate stand.
But two yards of land were all you wanted.

The Dwarf had taken three steps, undaunted;
Chittagong was claimed when holy flames fanned.
Every inch of her soil was sacred.

Your shattered heart and poetry pleaded,
Yet your grave was dug in a foreign land.
But two yards of land were all you wanted,
Every inch of her soil was sacred.

Note:
The First War of Indian Independence (1857) was fought in the name of the poet-emperor, Bahadur Shah Zafar (d. 1863). Two sons and a grandson had their heads displayed on a Delhi gate – now called *Khooni Darwaza* (Bloody Gate). Other royal males were also killed and the emperor exiled to Rangoon.
Granted three steps of land, Vishnu's Dwarf avatar took Earth, Heaven and Hell. A Sufi saint wrested Chittagong from demons by asking for as much land as would be lit by his lamp.

Full Moon Over Compton Verney

Seduced by white rock,
full moon descends, drunkenly
leaning on pine tree.

Haiku

Willow leaf hands hide
shivering naked branches:
monsoon winds whistle

Haiku

Poinsettias glow
poignant as Christ's bleeding heart
on my festive card.

Peach Blossoms

Peach blossoms in spring,
promising fruit in autumn.
For now I savour
confetti petals showered
like there were no tomorrow.

My Friends: Basir and Simon

Two intelligent friends and, of old wine, full measure,
a book, a garden corner and a little leisure ...
            – Shamsuddin Mohammed Hafiz

You wished for flagons of fine wine, Hafiz;
            a little leisure, one book – such riches!
You wished for a corner of a garden, Hafiz;
            but 'two friends' began your list of wishes.

Then envy me my two good friends, Hafiz.
            They flow from mellow East and feisty West
to fill my questing cup of joy, Hafiz.
            They're my wondrous book, my garden of rest.

A Fistful of Mud

A fistful of mud enters Gopal's mouth of mischief,
            but Mother Yashoda stops him from swallowing.
She peeks into a toothless grin where all cosmic space
            with suns and moons and planets is revolving.

Note:
The baby Krishna was called Gopal and Yashoda was his foster mother.

111

I Just Came By

(with thanks to William Carlos Williams
for 'This is Just to Say')

I just came by
to look you up,
to say I'm around,

to feel needed,
to say you matter,
that together

we can do anything;
but you were not alone;
someone else had dropped by

to borrow a cup of sugar
or coffee, to say 'Hi',
when I came by.

Namaskar: New Poems

Namaskar, Sir Walter

(in memory of my *Dadus*: Rai Sahib S N Chatterjee and Sri P N Mukherjee)

Namaskar, Sir Walter, I bring greetings from both my *Dadus*,
grandfathers from the Raj, retired pushers of fountain pens,
whose grand and innocent dreams you fed and fired.

My *Dadus*, paternal and maternal, I distinguished between them.
One was my Timarpur *Dadu*, blind but knowing every tree and
pothole
of the dusty Old Delhi neighbourhood where unneighbourly Timur
once pitched his city of tents and where later conquerors built offices
which were, he said, the new temples that fed our stomachs.
My grizzle-haired bespectacled Mussoorie *Dadu*, lived evergreen
in the hills and each summer I would visit him in his 'English' cottage
with its rambling rose briars. I would visit all his neighbours too,
but go most often to the childless major whose Scottish wife
lured us children with her doughnuts, tartans and apple cheeks.

No two *Dadus* were so unlike, but your brave words lit up their shelves;
they roamed with you in the craggy Highlands, the buzzing Borders,
the great castles and, of course, the regal streets of Edinburgh.

Courteous Timarpur *Dadu* had worked in Defence and earned a title.
My sister sampled his sacred snuff on his four-poster bed and I blew
horns
and ruffled his snowy hair, pronouncing him 'a lovely boy' – my Ivanhoe.
He had all the *Waverley* novels – his sons grew up on their swashbuckle.
My sister, cousins and I would stroke the fading embossed gold,
turn the yellow termite-nibbled pages, and Timarpur was transformed.
We roamed with you in the craggy Highlands, the buzzing Borders,
the great castles and, of course, the regal streets of Edinburgh.

Mussoorie *Dadu*, blunt and restless, took me rambling on long walks.
He wielded his walking stick like some antique sword. His tongue too

was a blade: heavy and damaging at times like an old broadsword
or darting light with rapier thrusts, but always sharp and sparkling.
His dogged brilliance in Income Tax had won his rulers' grudging
respect.
A juggler with numbers and words, he had your prodigious memory,
your love of books and travel and history. He gave me poems of
passion
and adventure – a free soul, my wild Gallic Rover, my young
Lochinvar.

Having roamed with you in the craggy Highlands, the buzzing
Borders,
the great castles and, of course, the regal streets of Edinburgh,
I stand at last before your statue. *Namaskar*, Sir Walter,
from the bottom of my heart. Please accept these Indian greetings.

Note
Timarpur: literally 'city of Timur', it is a part of Old Delhi.

Papaya Proud

Sprouted on Grandpa's papaya tree,
I grew green and oval, pouting proud.

Now I am magnolia ripe
and know where babies come from.

A Winter's Morning in Timarpur

The black and white cat snoozes in the play of light and shade
on the carport's tin roof, under the crumbling mango tree;
tail twitching, it dreams of plump pigeon and tender blue tit.
The scent of a hilsa fish curry floats from the kitchen window;
infiltrates its dream and teases it awake till it yawns and blinks.
A family of sparrows hop in the pomegranate tree:
twittering delight at the young green of its leaves,
playing among the orange of its buds.
Frenzied bees weave among white lemon flowers
and crimson frangipani fragrance the air.
High on a branch of the drumstick tree a tailor-bird's nest swings
in the November breeze, fresh with a hint of henna coolness.
The coral-stemmed white *shefali* flowers make *alpona* patterns
as they fall on the dew-damp grass.
The hibiscus still droops in prayer
to the early morning sun, its double petals
luscious red like much-kissed bridal lips.
A squirrel mother and child stir in their telephone-box nest
and milkmen balance heavy canisters on bicycle bars.
The roadside *chaiwalla* lights his charcoal fire *biri*
and the newsboy flings, with practised ease,
a rolled *Hindustan Times* to the third floor verandah.
Trucks and buses piled with raw produce and day labour
thunder imperially down the Grand Trunk Road
from the conquered pastures of Punjab and Haryana.
The black and white cat shadow boxes a Tiger Swallowtail
as a sleepy corner of Old Delhi wakes – and stretches.

Notes
alpona: a Bengali word for patterns drawn on the floor to welcome guests.
chaiwalla: someone who sells tea.
biri: a cheap Indian 'cigarette'.

117

An 'Indian Summer'

September – and I see the urban fisher-folk
dreaming of salmon leaping in roaring rivers.

Sunday in Sheffield – and I walk by the canal.
The high Himalayas drum with roaring rivers.

The dragonfly flits in the Yorkshire afternoon
while Mandakini descends in roaring waters.

Once a laughing goddess roamed along these banks;
now unknown, her name resounds through roaring waters.

Ducks swim, ruffling their feathers over this landscape.
Yards away, industry storms its roaring waters.

Whatever she is called, Ganga meditates
on Summer rippling the calm of English rivers.

Note
Mandakini is the name of the River Ganges when it is said to flow in Heaven.
Like the Ganges, many English rivers too, including those in Sheffield, were
worshipped as goddesses in pre-Christian times.

Swanning In

Saraswati, you come swanning in, smooth
as ever on your gliding bird, playing
your goddess self and expect me to rise
           and honour you.

An unexpected guest, you never knock
at my mind's door. You fly in with élan
and chat like it was yesterday. Any
           window will do.

This is no neighbourhood in India,
nor is this Heaven, but you are at home
no matter where; folding white wings – your bird
           swans into view.

While great Brahma rests, you are the blossom
on his six eyes, his heart-strumming music.
But each polyglot lilt you sing to me
           has an echo

that belongs to your raucous bird. 'Beauty,'
it winks, 'has an ugly voice, serpentine
like my neck.' Your company has a price,
           so I bow low

and make the most of any arrival.
Lady, I would put aside life itself,
if you would understand my need to hold
           when you let go.

Saraswati, you do not see the glint
in your bird's slanted eyes – a mortal dart.
Cushioned on airy clouds, impregnable,
           you breathe incense.

Even in Fortress Britain where I draw
my mind's portcullis and double-glaze all
windowpanes, you surprise me with your sudden
        gracious presence.

Ringing the alarm about intruders
would have no effect. By the time help came
you would be long gone; a few swan feathers
        for tantalising evidence.

Note:
Saraswati, wife of Brahma the Creator, is the Goddess of Music and the Arts.
The swan is her symbol.

Rain

When the heavens drenched the earth,
there were those who said that,
rumbling Vedic mantras,
Indra poured down oblations.

Others spoke of Indrani's tears,
showering both joy and sorrow;
or even Indra's winged elephant,
splashing and sporting while bathing.

(Airavata did incline
to ecstatic cleanliness.)
But Indra shook his royal head:
'Sometimes it *is* just rain I send.'

Note:
In Indian mythology, Indra, the King of the gods, causes thunder and rain, and
rides on a white winged elephant – Airavata. Indrani is his Queen.

The Sun Has Not Risen

The British sun has not risen
on this bleak February noon.
It sets, like *maya*,
spectacular on an empire
of Turner galleries. Skeletal trees
loom, like Lowry men, in the gloom –
gaunt old-timers with shaking limbs.
Grey buildings droop on ash-wet streets
where speckled salt bites in soufflé peaks,
crocus shoots are muffled in mulch.

Smothered in an anonymous
duffle-coat, I brave the harsh air.
Not even a card robin splashes
its melody of Christmas coral.
But on a lone bush the bloodstain
of poinsettia flames kindle
cindered memories till I feel
another sun bless my bowed head
and, to a veena's *raag*, I hear
my mother tongue singing to me.

Note:
In some Eastern philosophies the world is *maya* or illusion. A veena is a stringed
instrument associated with the Hindu Goddess of Music and the Arts. *Raag* is
notation in Indian music.

'Oliver Cromwell's Good Wife'

My friends, I beg thee to pray for me,
for mine is a great and honourable burden.
One rants and raves and petitions for annulment
when one's wedded spouse takes
some other lady to bosom
or commits gross bigamy.
At the very least one nags one's lawful spouse
and, by select neglect, discomforts him;
or complains to friends and basks in their sympathy;
or, if one has a mind to, indulges in fantasy
about torments to inflict on him if one only could –
for all would abhor such actions that run contrary
to God's laws and prove man's bestial frailty.
In another age, if all else failed,
then I could get me to a nunnery.
But none such expediency, alas, can solace me
– and more shame on me for thinking thus –
for he is a most righteous man and godly
who constantly reminds me of my beholden duty
and daily bids me join him in humble prayer
for my rival's welfare and long-lived success.
My friends, I beg thee to pray for me,
for he, in troth, is wedded to the Commonwealth
though all still name me 'Oliver Cromwell's good wife'.

The Last Mountain

Once we mountains sported wings,
soared proud above the heavens,
frolicked among fleecy clouds
and slid up and down the rainbows
that groaned with our mighty weight.
Rushing wind was our element;
we played the music of the spheres.
The sky gifted us a giddy lightness
that stole the breath away.
But we took our freedom for granted
and jealous gods have clipped our wings.
Now distant thunder growls our grumbles
as my brothers and sisters tower in dreams
of how we once were monarchs of the air.
But I, the smallest of the mountains,
escaped the wrath of gods.
I hide in the frothing ocean and, sleepless,
I bide my time with folded wings.
The sea soil rumbles my secret songs
as I call to my family to take heart.
Their trust will strengthen me
and lift me up to strike a blow for our kind,
to fly up to the sun itself if need be,
to dance in our remembered freedom,
for faith, they say, moves mountains.

Note:
Mountains once had wings – according to Indian myths.

Lucrezia's Mirror

I am the mirror
of Lucrezia Borgia,
the doppelganger
of her venomous beauty.
My cold dark eyes stared
at the flame of tawny cheeks
and the tamed jungle
wilderness of raven locks.
She watched her subtle
tongue and hid her hungry thoughts,
confiding only
in her diary of glass.
Some speak of murder,
but I reflect, not magnify.
She despatched her men
with the survival instinct
of a Medici.
Medusa-like she froze me
in gilt and walnut
splendour of angels with wings,
chubby cherubim
sporting among foliage.
Study my circles,
concentric like Dante's worlds.
Here too there is Hell,
Heaven and earthly Limbo.
Lions and dragons
jostle wild boar in ornate
hunting scenery,
but there is no Diana
to raise a mirror
to Lucrezia Borgia.

My mistress has long
faded into the pages
of cloistered memory,
and marble could not
preserve her body ground to dust,
unholy relic
in a modern museum.
But once I held up
her myriad fashion masks:
her roles of schemer,
daughter, sister, mistress, wife.
My face of metal
forged around a brittle pool
was the cauldron where
she stirred her poison potions.
Made in Ferrara,
I view the flawed and shifting globe.
I give a moment's
panic and titillation
as you behold me
and speculate on the dead.
I offer you hints,
abundant in my carvings:
trace the skeleton above,
the sly faun below.
They guard my transparency.
Beware of diving
beneath my antique surface
and discovering
a doppelganger,
not your own but Lucrezia's
glass-shattering shock.

Note:
This poem was inspired by Lucrezia Borgia's mirror in the 'Precious Exhibition'
at the Millennium Galleries in Sheffield in summer 2001.

Merlin's Sister

Merlin, you disowned me –
Morgana, your sister.
Arthur won't marry me,
although Mordred's mother.

Yours was the wizardry
that you said was better
than my failed witchery,
but *I'll* be the richer.

My son will seize the throne
and punish his father,
succeed to all we own;
he is *all* our future.

Interludes

Not a beginning, not an end,
this neutral place
is rich with stillness,
with movement in all directions.
In the words of the prophet, we
are travellers. So pass in peace, stranger,
though our orbits differ,
I too have rested here at these
limbo interludes
in our shared planet's rotation.
So catch your breath and let my words
welcome you like a friend's blessing.
May this space around you expand
and glow in the warmth of knowing
that it's only a corridor;
not a beginning, not an end,
but a green oasis.

A Birthday Kiss for Simon
(*For Simon Fletcher*)

Your birthday, Simon,
was an auspicious day for us
to drop in on the Scousers in Liverpool,
ghazal-*ustad* Basir, you and I,
from Manchester, Shrewsbury and Sheffield,
to break a leg – as they say –
only our one voice would carry us
in a *mushaira* in three tongues.

I'd packed a present for you –
a book of verse, what else?
My bag also held the green pin
with a smiley face that my Brian,
grown more Irish with the years,
sent you. Smile, Simon,
smile, it's your birthday.

I smiled to myself – my train
passed Warrington Central –
should I give you a kiss,
though I'm not one for kissing?
Perhaps, I thought. I knew you
long enough and well enough.
And yours was a birthday
when one needs the prop of friends.
At forty, you remain my junior,
and your mum says you don't look thirty.
It was okay to kiss the young,
a young friend on greeting,
especially on your birthday.

I panicked as the train
approached Liverpool Lime Street.
My silk sari rustled, upbraiding me:

127

how could I, sari-clad, kiss a man
not my husband? In a sari
I would not kiss even Brian in public –
and God knows how kissable he can be!
My sari like a silk glove packed
the punch of my Indian austerity.

I saw you waiting at the platform.
We waved. "Happy birthday, Simon!"
I kissed your cheek.
You were pleased I'd remembered.
The book, the pin, exchanged hands,
smiles connected.

A year later I offer this poem.
May each year bring you this good day
in Liverpool or Lahore, Manchester or Mumbai.
Smile, Simon, smile green on each birthday.

Notes
ghazal-*ustad*: a master of the ghazal form of poetry.
mushaira: a gathering of poets.

Postcard from Lilliput

Much news but
little space
on Lilliput
cards, so use
imagination.
Gulliver

Modern Times

CHINESE PUZZLE

This great wall was built
to bar the barbarian.
Now flock tourist hordes.

T.V. TURN ON

T.V. is today's
dominatrix: it whips us
to keep us turned on.

INTERNET MEDITATION

Zap through cyber-space
till the computer crashes.
Blank screen – space out time…

In-House

```
        we
    are  good  at
    keeping    things
    in-          house
    most          acci
    dents          hap
    pen             in
    the           home
    most           vio
    lence         takes
    place           in
    the           home
    we              are
    safe  as  houses.
```

Of Tongues and Amazons

Elocution class at the convent
was a heart-thumping ordeal for us 'native' girls.
Miss Rhondo would stride in,
a dark and miniscule dinosaur
who froze the grey matter in our brains
and delivered a vicious lockjaw
to cause our tongues to slither and stutter,
and our sweaty red-socked feet to shuffle
in white-chalked canvas shoes.
We rose in uniform drudgery
and greeted her with a singsong
'Good afternoon, Miss Rhondo' of shabby hypocrisy.
It irked her from the start
and she'd have us practise standing up
and sitting down with pathetic
time-wasting rows of 'Good afternoon'.
The crowd-saving distraction of 'the Mexican wave'
was not yet invented, but ripples of frustration
erupted and died.

Gita was surely a native too, but with attitude –
the one we looked up to with horror
and mounting excitement. No one knew
what she'd do on any given day
to break the regimented monotony.
She was a dusky native, but not like any of us;
she was an Amazon – tall and strong,
hockey Captain of our class.
'How dare you, Girl!' Miss Rhondo
thundered. 'You disgust me
with your native English.' But Gita's eyes
would dance mischief as she tossed
plump pigtails in the air.
She was always punished but she didn't care.

Amazons were from another world.
They belonged with Greek myths,
opium-eating Quincy's essays
and *Lamb's Tales From Shakespeare.*
In Miss Rhondo's elocution class
our Babu English weighed us down
with centuries of mangling
by sepoys and government clerks,
and we mutinied without meaning to.
Our wilting tongues, like orphaned Oliver,
asked for more. Miss Rhondo rattled
the marbles of sarcasm in our Indian mouths
with native tongues colliding:
Bengali, Punjabi, Sindhi, Tamil, Gujarati ...
tongues that won us punishment
when overheard on the playground.
'Please, Sister Katherine, Usha used Hindi
five times today.' 'Kamala is cursing
in Punjabi, Mother.' Only the mother tongue
knows the enchantment of cursing.
And how can we tell a friend a story
that does not end: *'Amar golpoti phurolo*
– noté gaachhti murolo ...'?
We ratted on each other like Nazi collaborators
and strangled our ancestral tongues
till they rose to haunt us in nightmares.

I was an 'assassin of the Queen's language',
Miss Rhondo said. There was blood
on my barbarous tongue. I looked at it
in the mirror – it was a 'native' tongue
that I had to use as a pummelling bag;
I had to tongue-punch it daily.
It was the protean dough of roti
for routine squeezing and thumping,
the gum that had to be sucked
and chewed and blown up into a bubble,
like igniting a hydrogen bomb.

131

Do not ask me which is more my own –
I shape the tongue as best I can
and language made me.

Gita was one of us 'natives', and yet one of a kind.
One summer's day with the ceiling fan blowing
Miss Rhondo's hot words around the room,
our tongues wilted, browbeaten into grinding submission.
Then Gita whistled! How she whistled!
No lady ever did that.
But Gita didn't care to be a lady and we knew
that Amazons live by different rules.
Miss Rhondo could not believe her ears.
'Who made that dreadful noise?' she asked
and we all knew but no one snitched.
She punished us all – we stood on benches,
holding up our schoolbags and feeling fools,
though for once we didn't care.
Honestas ante honores – 'honesty first, then glory',
Miss Rhondo reminded us. Our national anthem
said it too in a still more ancient tongue:
Satyameva jayaté – 'Truth triumphs'.
The truth was that Gita shrugged her shoulders
and we decided to join her that day.
We couldn't do what she had done
– we all aspired to ladyhood
– but we could join her for just one lesson
in standing on the benches, we would all
be punished as natives together,
though our mutiny could not last.
Gita, we knew, was an Amazon;
while we could only pretend,
she lived by other rules.

Note:
'*Amar golpoti phurolo – noté gaachhti murolo* ...', meaning 'My tale has ended
– the plant has wilted', is the beginning of a nonsensical rhyme that traditionally
ends a Bengali folktale.

The Nishi's Call

Its call is the sound of hot molasses syrup,
of ripest mango and candyfloss tenderness.
It stalks the streets and passes below your window;
it stops outside your door and moans its wild distress.

It can sound like your loving mother, passed away,
or your dead father who once held you to his chest;
it can sound like your own sweet sister, brother, friend,
or your darling child, your nearest and your dearest.

Beware! The Nishi walks the night with piercing cry.
It's the most haunting creature you can imagine.
Don't answer the Nishi's call. It's a soul-snatcher
and your voice is a silver cord it will reel in.

The Nishi carries an empty earthen vessel
to trap your soul if you answer its tempting cry.
When morning comes the Nishi's dead will rise again,
so close your mouth and ears or you will surely die.

A creature of night and of nightmares, the Nishi
stalks the streets and holds vigil below your window.
Its call is the sound of candyfloss tenderness.
Do not answer for it will snatch your soul and go.

Note:
The Nishi is part of Bengal's folklore. A creature of the night, it gathers the souls
of the unwary, deceiving them by calling in a familiar voice.

Our Lady of the Wayside Grotto

Your robe's cerulean folds
don't flutter in the wind,

but are lifted to wipe
the squirrel's whiskered face

as it washes itself –
a splash of red on blue.

The tilt of your draped head
speaks of modest prayer;

it rests the lone magpie
that remembers its mate

too loved this shrub-edged haunt –
black and white, life and death.

Your arms, spread in a wide
embrace of city air,

drip dewdrop blessings on
a mushrooming coppice

that guards your sacred space
in a wayside grotto.

Lady, the grass that grows
at your hidden feet sings

each season's hosannas
yards from the tarmac road

and bluebells peal praises
that ring endlessly true.

Our Lady, full of grace,
stand vigil by our world.

DARLING STOP

DARLING — STOP — CAN'T FIND UNDERWEAR —-
STOP — COME BACK — STOP — JACK

DARLING — STOP — EXAMINE CUPBOARD —-
STOP — THEN HEAD — STOP — JILL

DARLING — STOP — RETURN URGENT —-
STOP — DIVORCE IMMINENT — STOP — JACK

DARLING — STOP — JILL

When the Beast Cried

When the Beast cried
the Beauty's last defence was gone.
When the Beast cried
innocence and revulsion died.
With new insight she looked upon
his rough features. Her love was won
When the Beast cried.

More Than I Wear
(for the young women in the Asian Women's Resource Association)

A young woman, Asian and British,
I have swallowed the world's rough oyster
       – pearl and all; yes, pearl and all.

I've had hard times and will face worse times,
but my gear is sorted and, sister,
       right now, I'm having a ball!

I move to Indi-pop and bhangra,
dupatta flying from my shoulder
       – angel wings and waterfall.

       The world is my oyster – pearl and all.
       Sister, right now, I'm having a ball!

Dadiji gave me this hand-stitched *chunni*.
Her love flows through it like a river,
       and I float tall – I float tall.

       The world is my oyster – pearl and all.
       Sister, right now, I'm having a ball!

I bought myself this denim jacket
and embroidered a lotus flower
       – there's none like it in the mall!

       The world is my oyster – pearl and all.
       Sister, right now, I'm having a ball!

My silk *kameez* glows with gold sequins
my satin *salwar* mirrors the hour
       in Halifax and Bengal.

The world is my oyster – pearl and all.
Sister, right now, I'm having a ball!

My Doc Martins pack a feisty kick.
I am from Bradford and Jullunder,
        Mirpur, Punjab and Walsall.

        The world is my oyster – pearl and all.
        Sister, right now, I'm having a ball!

I'm more than I wear: Asian British.
My clothes are those that eye the future,
with respect for tradition's power.
Sari or jeans, I am the daughter
        of Birmingham and Southall.

        The world is my oyster – pearl and all.
        Sister, right now, I'm having a ball!
        Sister, right now, I'm having a ball!

Not Goldilocks

With blonde hair cropped, I am not Goldilocks.
It's true I could not help but help myself
to Baby Bear's porridge – I wolfed it down.

In Mummy Bear's coat I am bear-hugged-warm
though I shiver into your Daddy Bear eyes.

Goldilocks trespassed in her childhood story
and, luckily, she got away lightly.

This bare tent offers fitful sleep tonight
- I must bear reality to survive.
What will tomorrow bring the refugee?

Home

When I left, my eyes caressed
each grieving street, each screaming rooftop.
The memory of my home
forever burnt into my smouldering heart.

And this place, this yawning lull
between firing zones, this nameless limbo
is a numbered shelter – for a while
of counting heartbeats – but it is not home.

This cursed space spawned my one surviving child:
mottled fruit of blasphemy, rare blossom of rape and rage.
It nurtured too the wild-eyed orphan
that still suckles at my shrivelled breast.

Now the nights of counting stars are done,
detailing a desperate history
of too many burnt and buried.
The powerful tire of carnage and the stench of blood,
now the talk is of amnesty
and rebuilding homes and lives.

I have packed our patchwork quilt,
gathered a handful of corn and my inheritance.
I have stopped their ignorant chatter of 'home'.
I have set this shack on fire. I count on no return.

'Children, watch it burn as we walk away.
Nothing is left here. We can go home at last.
This place was only a shelter through the dragging years –
a makeshift pain – it was never home.'

Today, as we turn to face the long march back,
I ache for the cool of welcoming streets and rooftops.
But the memory of this place is forever burnt
into my children's eyes and its cinders ignite my fear.